IF YOU SEE MY HUSBAND, WOULD YOU PLEASE SEND HIM HOME

Christian Families Can Survive Adultery

KAREN M. BUTLER

WALTON
PUBLISHING HOUSE

Walton Publishing House
Houston, Texas
www.waltonpublishinghouse.com
Printed in the United States of America

ISBN: 978-1-953993-30-4 (Paperback)

ISBN: 978-1-953993-29-8 (Digital/ E-book)

Dedication

"Ladies"

TABLE OF CONTENTS

Introduction - Mission

Many Christian marriages end in divorce due to adultery. I can say this because I experienced infidelity in my marriage in the tenth year. Although my marriage did not end in divorce, I understand firsthand the pain and betrayal that accompanies the act of adultery.

Since the beginning, God has always honored the covenant of marriage, regardless of how the secular world has tried to redefine what constitutes marriage. This covenant and commitment will never change. Marriage has always been a binding agreement between one man and one woman.

I was inspired to write this book for women who have been betrayed by adultery, which landed them at a crossroads in their marriage. Truly, I empathize with those of you who feel like giving up on your marriage; those of you who feel isolated and betrayed. Understandably, I realize you are crying out for help but can't find a safe place to turn and your ultimate trust has been shattered. *You are not alone.*

I remember being that woman and looking for someone to help me understand the pain I was feeling by the man I loved and trusted. He was the father of my adorable children. That amazing bond we once shared was shattered. After the betrayal, I felt like I wasn't ready to deal with the challenges ahead. Actually, I didn't think I was even capable of handling my new reality.

By God's grace, I was able to face my darkest moments. Today after being married for thirty-two years to my husband Robert, I would like to share some of our experiences and wisdom that helped us. It is my prayer that my story will help you through this difficult season of your life. We have worked extremely hard to rebuild our lives after recommitting ourselves to our marriage. I have forgiven him, and we have built a thriving marriage and ministry together.

This book will give you options on what to do after unfaithfulness has creeped into the relationship. During this book, I will share my story and give dynamic solutions to pull you through this season. It is my prayer that you find encouragement and even solutions to help you overcome this difficult time. This book is not to persuade you to stay and fight for your marriage and neither is it advocating for you to leave. At the end of our journey together, I want you to have the tools to allow the Holy Spirit to direct you in the best way for you to go. Surviving infidelity is never easy.

Preface

It's no secret that infidelity in Christian marriages is on the rise. It seems as if the indiscretions of infidelity are often kept in a dark closet to protect the guilty party or to save the faithful spouse from the embarrassment of having to admit an affair. Sadly, there are far too many women experiencing the effects of a cheating spouse. In fact, statistics tell us that 20% of married men admitted to having sex with someone who is not their spouse while married.[1] It makes you wonder, *do all men cheat?*

---

[1] Wendy Wang, "Who Cheats More? The Demographics of Infidelity in America," Institute for Family Studies, January 10, 2018, https://ifstudies.org/blog/who-cheats-more-the-demographics-of-cheating-in-america, (accessed 12/5/21)

CHAPTER ONE

Where Art Thou?

I t was spring of 2000 and everything in my life seemed out of balance. No matter how hard I tried to manage all my responsibilities, I just couldn't get a grip on things. There were so many obligations pulling at me. The husband, my young children, and the expectations as a leader in my church were just some of the things that lobbied for my attention. To add more irons in the fire, I was running a successful daycare with a full staff. Although I had everything that a woman could ever need or even desire to be successful in managing a household, things didn't feel right for me. I couldn't help but wonder, w*hy am I feeling so frustrated?*

One day, I felt it all start to come crashing down and I immediately began to feel disconnected to my husband. I remember that day as if it were yesterday. I stood in my exquisitely designed kitchen in one of the suburbs of Maryland, in our custom built home, asking my husband if he had ever been unfaithful to me. His immediate response, of course, was no, but for some odd reason, I just didn't believe his answer. As women, our intuition senses when possible betrayal has surfaced.

But I didn't know where these feelings of insecurity were

coming from as there was nothing I could pinpoint. On the outside we were *The Butlers*, the couple that everyone adored and sought out for advice. We were leaders in our local church and in the community and lived the dream life that many would envy.

However, that day whatever stench was lurking out of his 'feigned' closet hit me like a freight train, and suddenly I became very irritable for no reason. I was unable to focus on even the smallest tasks and an uncomfortable feeling sat within the pit of my stomach. Suddenly, my husband seemed like a stranger to me in our home.

Strangely as I was battling with this emotional overwhelm, he was being extremely quiet and very helpful. There was a wicked silence in the atmosphere of the home. I knew my spouse. Something had taken place that I didn't know about. Something was happening to our once rock-solid marriage, but what was it? Whatever it was it caused me to lose my appetite for food without reason.

I had to get out of there, and quickly. It was the perfect time to escape to the annual National Conference for Women held at Disney World that was scheduled in just a few days. I had to make a decision whether or not to fly out and let my husband take care of the children for a couple of days. I only had two days and I quickly made a decision to fly out.

Before leaving, my intuition prompted me to ask him if he had ever been unfaithful to me.

"Robert, have you had thoughts about cheating on me? Are you happy in our relationship?" I questioned.

"Why would you ask me a question like that?" he snapped back.

"I'm not sure."

"Would you tell me the truth, if so?" I further inquired.

"I love you Karen," was his response.

During the flight, I meditated on our busy lives and the questions I had asked Robert. Deciding to leave for my trip gave me an opportunity to soul search. I figured the conference would keep me too busy to think about the strangeness I was experiencing. It would be good to escape and connect with my old friends.

The first day of the conference was monotonous as usual. A bit later, I met a couple of young ladies, Latoya and Grace. We sat at the same table and had an open discussion about the political aspects of business.

"So, what's your name again?" Latoya asked.

"Karen Butler. I'm from Maryland, where seafood is the greatest," I said with a warm smile. "Latoya, where are you from?" I asked.

"North Carolina... Karen, would you like to go out to dinner with us tonight?" Grace asked.

"Sure" I responded.

"Great...meet us in the lobby at seven o'clock."

I returned to my hotel room, showered, and slipped into a cute, black, sleeveless, evening summer dress. It was close to seven o'clock when the phone rang. I didn't answer, thinking it was Robert. I did not want to be bothered with any more conversations about the concerns of our marriage. Besides, I was going out to have a wonderful evening.

The ladies were waiting for me in the lobby. "Hi, guys," I greeted enthusiastically.

"We're just waiting for the shuttle," Grace said.

After our transportation arrived, we headed to a quaint place inside the theme park and sat at a table outside of the restaurant. I ordered a deli club sandwich, while Grace and Latoya ordered salads. The dinner conversation started off great, we all had something in common in being married with children. This is always a good way of starting conversations. Latoya started with the fact of her being divorced and having three children.

"Two years ago, my husband had an affair with my neighbor. I was extremely angry. I could not believe he would be involved in such a degrading act. But anyway, I chose to divorce his butt so fast. Now we just share custody of our three children."

"Oh, Latoya, I'm so sorry," Grace said. "I know that had to be a horrible thing for you to go through."

"Yeah, and can you believe he never wanted me to leave the house? He probably just didn't want me to see what he was out there doing."

For some reason, this conversation seemed very uncomfortable for me to hear. I started to put myself in Latoya's place, wondering how I would feel if those shoes were on my feet. Grace and I sat compassionately listening to her with patience.

"This man took ten years of my life, just to end our marriage with my neighbor. A young, thin blonde! I was definitely much prettier than her," she continued.

"How did you deal with that devastation?" I asked.

"I wasn't alone. If I did not have Christ in my life, I would have probably hurt him and that woman. Nobody's faithful, the way I see it now. You never know what your spouse could be doing behind your back," she said. "The most peculiar thing happened prior to me finding out about the affair. I had a good idea that he wasn't faithful, but no true evidence."

Immediately, my heart dropped into my stomach. "Latoya, did

you ever consider trying to work the marriage out?" I asked.

"Sure, I have always wanted to salvage what could be saved. But the other woman would not even let him come up for air. He was very confused and afraid. At least, that's what he told me. He felt that he was caught, and life was over with me. I mean, he messed up. Some of these *strumpets* out here don't even give you a chance to work on your relationship if your man is tipping. Anyway, she persuaded him that she would give him a better life because she didn't have children and they would have a problem-free relationship. Now she's moved on to someone with a little more money. My husband couldn't support her compulsive shopping addiction. Don't forget, he had to pay child support."

"Well, my husband and I have been married for sixteen years," Grace said. "Yup, we have four children, and it hasn't always been easy, but we hung in there and gave it all we had. Karen, are you married?" she turned to me and asked.

"Yes, I am," I said. I thought to myself, *they are not going to get into my business.* "I've been married for ten years. I am definitely still working on the communication gap in our relationship. I'm sure you can give me some points on handling this," I said with a smirk.

"One of the mothers in the church always told me that if it can be fixed, fix it. If it can't, then pray about it," Grace said.

"How are your children adjusting to the divorce, Latoya?" I asked.

"They're doing alright," she responded. "Sometimes they really miss their father not being directly in the home. I'll get them a stepfather one day. My mom got one for me when her marriage went bad and for the last two years, I've just been playing around anyway. I don't really want a relationship, because they're just too complicated."

"We have to always remember no one is perfect, not even us. I've been married for sixteen years, and we haven't experienced adultery." With a soft tone, Grace said, "We have had other problems to work

5

through."

"You know, wouldn't it have been great if the other woman sent your husband back home where he belonged?" I asked while laughing.

"Yes, Karen, but that's like a serious fairytale."

"No, it could be a commitment between women." We started laughing until tears started to fall.

"Stop, guys, I'm for real. It will go something like this. Let's say that if a man is married, and a woman becomes aware that he's trying to come on to her that she doesn't entertain the possibility of having an adulterous relationship with him but will just send his butt home. Actually, ship him through UPS." We continued to laugh so hard. My stomach muscles started to become sore.

"We should attach a note on to his shirt that reads, *If you see my husband, would you please send him home!*"

"Karen, that is such a great idea," Latoya said. "He wouldn't have anybody to jump in the sack with but his little faithful wife. What a great idea, Karen," she said while still laughing. We all continued to chuckle. "Karen, there is one problem. I wish that this invention was discovered two years ago. Maybe we would still be together today."

"I know, Latoya. She shouldn't have had sex with him. She definitely should have encouraged him to go to his family."

"But Karen, that would be too good to be true," Latoya said.

"Admit it, some of these men in the church are off the chain, trying to justify that it's just a man thing. Believe it or not, some of them really think God meant for them to have numerous relationships," I said while laughing.

"I know, Karen. They have some religions that encourage more than one partner. How sick is that? Well, it always works out to the advantage of the male," said Grace.

6

"What if women said their Bible told them to go have sex with other men when they get tired of the one they married?"asked LaToya.

"That's funny," I said.

"No really, I don't think we are making these men accountable in our churches today for going off and starting new families," she explained.

"Well, my husband thought he had the right to do whatever he chose, because I allowed him to. But one day, I took that stand. I told him I would no longer live like this. It's not healthy for me or the children. I was always on edge about getting AIDS and other diseases. Don't forget, the statistics show that more and more married females are being exposed to HIV."

"You're right, Latoya," I said. "You shouldn't live in fear. But make sure you consider abstinence instead of multiple partners. Guys, I constantly ask for God's help in that area. I would like to have a prayer for our families," I said.

We held hands, and I asked God to heal any scars in our families.

"Please, God, continue to have mercy on us although our marriages may sometimes get off course. Reduce the divorce rates amongst the Christian community. Thank you God, for your hedge of protection around us. Amen.

Now, who's ready for dessert?" I ended.

After dessert, we walked around the theme park. It seemed as if we were high-school buddies hanging out. The park was bright and cheerful. This was definitely a girls' night out. I almost forgot what that felt like - just talking to other women and sharing life's experiences. We did not have a depressing pity party about our mates nor did we allow ourselves to become upset with the state of marriages. We decided to enjoy the moment. Sometimes you just need someone to talk to who will not judge you because of your stand with God.

Listening to one another's concerns on how to make good decisions in a contaminated marriage and letting my hair down was very much needed, and I laughed and had such a pleasant time with the girls.

When I went back to the hotel room, my dear husband had called and left a message on the recording. He again sounded like he was walking on eggshells.

"Hi, honey," he said. "Just wanted to see how things were going down there in Disney World."

Hearing his voice made me hurt. Why did it seem like he lied to me? I really didn't know what was going on, but my heart immediately started pounding. "Please call me back. I need to hear from you tonight."

I lit my lavender candle and read one of my favorite books. Before I knew it, I had to blow out the candle and go off to sleep in order to wake up by six o'clock am. Starting to feel extremely exhausted, I laid there imagining what it would be like without Robert beside me forever. I snapped out of it. *This is crazy. Why do I keep thinking like this?*

CHAPTER TWO

> *"Can a Man Take Fire in His Bosom and Not Get Burned?"*
> *Proverbs 6:27 KJV*

The trip quickly came to an end and I flew back home on my return flight. When the plane landed, Robert was waiting in front of baggage claim. When I saw him, he had a dark cloud over him. I knew something was wrong. For the first time, I no longer had the desire to be married anymore. This seemed to be so crazy to me, but my skin was curling as he embraced me. I tried not to show any signs of rejection or discomfort.

"How was the trip?" he asked.

"Um, it was alright," I responded.

He grabbed my things and we headed to the car. The first few minutes were completely silent as we drove home. In the rear view mirror I glanced at the kids who were sleeping in the back seat.

"Is everything going okay?" he asked.

"No. Not really."

I just didn't know how to express what was wrong without being accusatory so I attempted to keep my response short. I must say, when you are in a relationship, it is very difficult to expect the unexpected. So, I was hoping that what I felt in my spirit was wrong.

When we arrived at the house, Robert took the bags upstairs and dropped them onto the bed. He was so overdue for intimacy but I had no desire. He stared at my body as I walked across the bedroom floor. There was such a chilling silence in the room.

"Robert, I want to ask you a question, and please do not lie. I have had an unexplainable infection. It could just be a common yeast infection but I'm not sure. As a matter of fact, I'm starting to feel very different about you. Have you ever been with another woman?"

I was expecting him to embrace me and say, "No. I could never do that to you."

He paused and looked down at the floor.

"Karen, I never intended to hurt you." He surprisingly responded.

I couldn't believe what I was hearing.

"Just tell me the truth!" I said as my voice began to escalate and I became enraged.

Holding his head down, he answered, "I'm sorry. I love you."

Oh my goodness. I was in disbelief. I wanted him to tell me 'no' just to spare me from the trauma. My entire world shifted in that one moment.

"What?!!! Why? Who is she? How could you?" I yelled out.

"When I married you, I handed my heart over. How could you do this to someone you truly love? My love has never stopped growing for you, honey. When did this happen?" I added.

"It was a bad mistake that I made. I guess about two weeks ago," he responded as he looked at me with embarrassment and hurt in his eyes.

I didn't care about his guilt. I wanted him to feel even guiltier. The act had been committed and there was nothing that could be done to fix how I was feeling in that moment.

"You know what I think? Men must really have similar characteristics to dogs."

A burst of tears suddenly came streaming down my face like Niagara Falls. Anger and rage rose up within me. It felt like someone had just told me a loved one had died. I hoped I was just dreaming. Totally numb standing on my feet, I didn't know what to do next.

How could this happen to me? I had been so faithful in the relationship. I really did not deserve such calamity. My life, which was once full of joy and laughter, was just destroyed by a man who didn't handle me with care.

I couldn't stop pressing him. I wanted him to feel the pain, the hurt and the disappointment that I felt in the pit of my stomach. I wanted him to feel the dirtiness I felt as I looked at him, wanting to put my hands on him.

"This is called foul living. I choose not to live in a shattered-covenant relationship. Is this an ongoing affair?" I questioned.

"No, Karen. As weak as it may sound, I got caught up in a stupid moment. I am so sorry! Please forgive me! Please!"

How could he ask for forgiveness? I had a God-given right to expect an adultery-free marriage. If this was a difficult task for him, he must not truly have been the one. Crying like a sobbing infant who missed her timed feeding, the betrayal was starting to become a true reality. As Robert sat like a confused puppy, my anger grew

11

unbearably out of control.

This was all too much for me to bear. I decided at that moment that for the first time in our relationship, it was going to be all about me if I decided to continue. I was torn and angry. What excuse could he possibly have given me for this betrayal? I wanted answers!

Standing there, I needed to process what he had confessed to. There were so many thoughts that raced through my head. Even though there was no justification in what had taken place, I made a quick decision to discontinue all of my responsibilities that would create a comfortable and secure home for Robert. Adultery is a very serious problem and it needs to be addressed immediately.

I snapped out of it for a moment as I thought about the infection I was dealing with. I had no idea what my body could have been exposed to, so I rushed to the emergency room to get tested for any type of STD. I wasn't really thinking straight at that time because I could have waited until Monday to go to my private doctor, but I just had to know what was going on. This situation consumed my mind, thoughts, and reasoning with all sorts of thoughts racing through my mind.

What if I were exposed to AIDS? Who would take care of my children?

Crying all the way to the closest hospital, I thought my life would be over. Life throws challenges that you are in no way prepared for. This was the biggest and hardest challenge I had ever faced. I just didn't understand how this could have happened to me...to us. We had a Christian marriage. We prayed together, we served God together and we were raising our children to do the same. *What happened? What had I missed?* I knew Robert loved the Lord, but how could something like this happen?

The Bible speaks of a woman being a helpmeet to her husband. I have always believed she should help out wherever there's a need to establish a strong family. I thought I was doing exactly what I was supposed to do by being a faithful wife. The thought of me working to set up one of the most lucrative businesses and Robert's seeming to be ungrateful was so disappointing. All of the sacrifices I made of myself, children, and friends to build the business and the life we were able to enjoy were so unfair. Everything I did, I did with us in mind. I thought and planned when everyone else was asleep. How could his thoughts have been on a totally different page?

Finally arriving at the Emergency Room, I checked in and told the registrar that I needed all possible tests to determine if I was exposed to any sexual diseases. Tears of pain ran down my cheeks. The receptionist held my arm and tried to comfort me. As I was feeling like I was having an anxiety attack, the nurse finally called my name.

"Karen Butler," she said.

I thought to myself, *here we go!* I felt so alone at that moment. I asked myself, *where is God?*

I walked down a long hall to get to the patient's room. "Please take off your clothes and put this gown on open to the back," she said.

"The doctor will be in shortly."

The room was so cold. I just asked God to let everything be alright.

The doctor entered. She was a petite, middle aged woman displaying a gentle smile.

"Hi, my name is Dr. Musik. What seems to be the problem today?"

Feeling emotionally wrecked, I said that my husband had a one-night stand and I wanted to be checked for any diseases.

"Well, let's take some tests. We also need to take blood work." With water still streaming down my face, I agreed.

She proceeded with the examination as I lay there looking at the ceiling with more tears streaming down my face.

"From examining you, everything looks fine, but we'll know more when the results come back in a couple of days."

"Oh no, I don't think I can wait that long." Feeling like I was going crazy, I burst into tears again and thanked her for her help.

Dr. Musik comforted me by saying, "Unfortunate situations do happen. You'll be alright. Just don't think of the worst."

"Thank you doctor," I said.

"Try not to worry about this too much," she said, as if I could adhere to that advice at that moment.

Still in a state of shock, having had the thought of being exempt from adultery obliterated, I felt numb in every nerve in my body. In contrast, as Christians sometimes we have a false sense of reality that calamity should bypass our door. It would be great, but we do have tests and trials to overcome and none of us are exempt. Faithful people experience unfair situations. But through it all, beyond any circumstance, our God is always with us.

I left the hospital in a state of confusion. My body felt weak, and the tears just wouldn't stop flowing. Driving down the highway, I knew I needed someone to talk to before I lost my mind. So, I stopped by a friend's house. She answered the door in shock at the state I was in. I was always the strong friend that everyone came to with their problems. I would hold them in my arms as they sobbed or vented about their life's circumstances. But that wasn't usually me. I was conservative and private about anything I was going through.

However, this time I couldn't hide the pain. Very tearfully, I told Jen that my husband had an affair. She was shocked.

"This is unbelievable. You have been so good to him. How could he? You are so pretty! Men are dogs," she said angrily.

"No, Jen. They are God's creatures. They are very different from us, but not dogs. I just don't want to think that way. Besides, everything that God made was good," I said sadly.

"Well, you're a better woman than I, because there is no good that can come from something such as this."

"Jen, you're making me feel worse."

"Wake up, Karen! It's over! You can take care of the kids because you have a business. I feel he decided to give up on your marriage when he made that decision to be unfaithful."

I started to cry again. "I am so confused right now. It is hard for me to decide whether or not to divorce. I have to go, Jen. Thanks for talking." I stormed out of her front door and rushed to the car.

My heart felt like it was bleeding. It was difficult to make a lifetime decision while my emotions were all over the place. Having been in a daze for a period of time, the process was so hard. Where would I start? I needed to make a thorough decision about staying. But how could I decide when there was so much to consider? The children, homes, cars, investments—it was all so overwhelming to even think about working out the details for separation.

I headed home to face him.

When I pulled into my driveway, the children ran over to the car to greet me with wide-stretched arms. "Mommy, where have you been? We missed you, and Daddy didn't know where you were," Lauren said.

"Have you guys eaten dinner?"

"Yes. We had spaghetti and meatballs," she said.

"Where is Daddy?"

"Upstairs in your room."

"Let's go inside to take baths."

I took the children into the house. After tossing my keys on the small table in the foyer, the children followed me upstairs to my bedroom to greet Robert.

"Hey," I said to Robert as I continued to engage with the kids.

"Okay, guys let's get ready for bath time."

The two girls rushed to their bedrooms to get toys to put in the bathtub while bathing.

I ran a bathtub of warm water for our baby boy and re-entered our bedroom.

"Karen, while you were gone, I had been thinking that I would do whatever it takes to save our marriage," he said.

"I don't think our marriage is salvageable," I said. "It is so painful thinking about you being with another woman after we have shared such good times and interests."

"Weren't we the best of friends? What went wrong? How did we end up on this page anyway? There are so many unanswered questions that I do not know who to go to for help," I said confusedly.

"Oh, the doctor's office called," Robert said. "They said for you to call as soon as possible."

First, I paused when Robert gently gave me the message from the

16

doctor's office. Then I called to get the results.

"Hello, my name is Karen Butler. I'm returning your call."

"Yes, Mrs. Butler. May I have the last four digits of your social security number?" After I provided the information the receptionist proceeded. "Your results were negative. You may want to follow up with Dr. Musik if you have any other concerns."

"Thank you." I said and hung up the phone. Although I was relieved, I still felt angry. All types of thoughts were going through my mind: people die from getting certain sexually transmitted diseases. I knew this was not something that could be taken lightly. Truthfully, I knew there was a long road to marriage recovery if I decided to stay.

Neither of us knew what to do next. During the next three weeks I didn't have an appetite, and started to lose weight. I'd lost ten pounds in the first week. The stress of the betrayal was taking control of my mind and body. I called my doctor and she said losing weight too fast is not safe.

I had to remember to eat. Robert would ask me if I wanted my different favorite foods to inspire me to eat small meals and that was helpful.

A few weeks after the adultery, Robert and I decided to seek counsel from an older couple who were our friends.

"Hi, Barbara. This is Karen."

"Hello, sweetie! How are you doing?" she asked.

"Well, I think I'll be okay. Robert and I have come into a serious crisis. Do you guys have anything planned for Friday evening?" I asked.

"We are free on Friday," Barbara said. "Would you guys like to go out for dinner?"

"Sure, maybe I can make some sort of sense out of this situation."

That Friday we met Tom and Barbara at a quaint restaurant in Greenbelt. The hostess escorted us to the reserved table for four. Robert and Tom pulled chairs from the table to seat me and Barbara. We immediately started catching up and talking about our children, church, and then there was a pause as we viewed the extensive menu.

The waitress came to the table to take our beverage order and returned with fresh baked bread. She asked, "Are you ready to order?"

"Yes, I'll have blackened salmon with a baked potato," I said.

Robert ordered a medium well-done filet mignon with mashed potatoes. Tom ordered Chicken Marsala for him and Barbara. We continued to talk about mutual topics until the food arrived. When we finished eating our dinner the waitress asked, "Are you ready for dessert?"

We all replied, "We're full, no thank you." She removed our plates and offered us coffee. "Sure, I'll have coffee," Tom responded.

"So how are you? What's wrong?" Barbara asked. For a moment I asked myself what am I doing? I thought our situation was becoming really confusing. I was vulnerable and so was Robert.

"I'll let Robert share the unfortunate circumstances with you because it's not for me to tell," I said softly.

"Well, I've made a huge mistake that can cost me my marriage. Karen is thinking about leaving. I had an affair," he said.

"Are you in love with this person Robert?" Tom asked.

"No. It was a one-night stand."

"You can make it through this," Tom said. "You are not by yourself. There are many others in worse situations. Robert, don't be so hard on yourself. I've been there myself."

"Tom, with no disrespect, you are assuming that I will automatically stay with him," I said. "I must forgive, but biblically, I am not required to stay in an adulterous relationship. This decision is solely up to me."

"Barbara, what did God bring you and Tom through?" I asked.

"Please just explain your problem and tell me how God brought you to the place where you are in your relationship now."

"Karen, I'm sorry. I won't share my story because I can't see where it will help you."

Deeply in disbelief that Barbara had the audacity to respond like that, I immediately knew we were wasting our time to get spiritual guidance from this couple.

Hurtfully, I responded, "Well, I really appreciate your poised relationship, as if you grew overnight, but you can't relate to my scars that I'm bearing right now. Stay cute. I'm going to seek real answers with real people." I got up from the table and ran to the front door toward our car. Robert ran behind me. I was crying again.

"Karen, wait!"

"No, I'm tired of everyone wearing a fake face and not helping with real life situations in the church." As Robert gracefully pulled my arm towards the table they were sitting at, I sat and listened to Barbara explain what she meant by saying her story would not help us.

However, she talked about love in a marriage and how to be faithful to one another.

19

"Will our marriage ever reach a monumental level of commitment or peace?" I asked Barbara.

"It can, but it will take hard work and commitment," she replied.

After they prayed with us, we thanked them and left the restaurant.

"Do you want to go to the Inner Harbor for a walk?" Robert asked. That was one of the places we would go on dates.

"No, I'm just ready to go home, honey" I said. When we got into our car I reclined my seat to slightly lean back in a comfortable mode.

After having that encounter with Bob and Barbara, I began to reminisce on how guarded some Christians can be. The thought came to my mind that the purpose of church is to become more like Christ. My mind continued to drift off to how challenging the future looked before us. After going into a deep thought, I realized that although you may not be led to share your experiences with others, remember, when a couple is experiencing infidelity, sometimes it's not about protecting your good reputation. It is about witnessing to help save marriages. I wish there were support groups in the churches for adultery. Nevertheless, when you go to God's house, you only see couples looking great together in various types of leadership. In contrast, I felt like no other person had experienced adultery. Adultery is so painful. You really do think there is no hope for marriage.

I still needed to find someone who could help me understand what I was going through. I needed someone to tell me everything would be okay. I needed someone to give me the tools to understand why I felt like an emotional roller coaster. *Would I ever be whole again? Could anyone help me save my bleeding heart?*

We turned to a few leaders in church, but no one could really

20

touch this situation. If only someone could have just told us how they overcame such a blow and how their relationship was glued back together, it would have helped me with my pain. I quickly realized that many people carry a burden like this alone. And many times, because they did not get the help they desperately needed, they ended up divorcing.

This is when I realized the church community is equipped to deal with other life issues but not adultery. I needed a support group, or a friend, or a mentor at the time because it would have helped me so much. Take any problem in your life. It is always easier when someone can relate to the experience you're going through. If there's a death in the family, everyone is so supportive. They share how they lost a loved one and what they did to have a healthy healing process. Why does it have to be so different when it comes to adultery?

Some time after that dinner I attended a women's conference. The keynote speaker asked the audience to bow their heads and close their eyes. Then she said, "if you have been molested as a child please stand, if you have been raped, please stand, if you have been in an unfaithful marriage please stand." When I stood up in sync to my adulterous marriage, I looked around and the room was full of broken people who needed some type of emotional support. The purpose of that exercise was to let women know that they're not alone, although they may feel like they're the only one standing.

"Thank you," the speaker said. There was a sound of unified soft tears in the midst. I realized that I was not alone. There was a room filled with women like me, who had experienced some type of trauma. Although we were standing for different reasons, we were unified in a moment of hurt.

So, then my question is, why don't we help one another? Why does it seem so difficult to find the support we need? I am not saying we should go around and spread our business to everyone, but it's good to have those that will help bear the burden when you don't know which way to turn. Some women are used to dealing with this type of thing, and for some it is completely new. Well, the conference was very refreshing. All of the ladies started embracing one another. There was no judgment, although we didn't know one another we formed an emotional and spiritual bond in that moment. I remember how empowered I felt leaving the conference. While driving back home the thought of my circumstances caused me to seek a plan of action. I wanted to have a conversation with him and the kids about us separating while I processed my life.

A few days passed and I asked Robert to meet with me one afternoon in the privacy of our home. We sat there in our oversized family room. The kids were upstairs playing in the playroom.

"I'm sorry, Robert. I don't think I can ever trust you again. How could you sleep next to me every night with this huge secret? Did you have any conscience at all? By the way, I did notice that you weren't volunteering in the church anymore." I didn't take a breath as each question rolled out one after the other.

"Karen, I have to get my home in order," he said confusedly.

At the moment I had a sheer level of respect and compassion for him to not allow this tragedy to go ignored. He was repentant, which gave me an option to stay or leave. The room was silent as we sat on our midnight blue, plush leather sofa outlined with silver nail heads. I proceeded further.

"The other day, I saw a gray shadow of a body leaving our bedroom," I said. "It was the spirit of a ghost; an unwelcome silhouette of a foul spirit had been in our bed."

He just sat calmly, seeming to be confused.

Robert, that ghost wasn't my imagination," I said. "As a matter of fact, the Holy Spirit let me know that the unclean spirit had to be removed from our home. Therefore, I thoroughly prayed throughout the home."

As we continued to sit, I shared with him that we all have various types of inadequacies and he's not the worst person in the world. He just made a very bad decision. Some decisions are more destructive than others, but each needs to be confronted. Marriage is definitely based on trust. In every sector of this unit, trust is vital. We sat in silence as the evening came near. I didn't know whether to forgive or separate.

Two days later Robert and I happened to be in the kitchen at the same time. He pulled my arm and tried to embrace me with a kiss. I rejected the embracement.

"I love you, Karen. I hope we can work this out. But if you choose to leave, you will be my wife forever. Just please try to forgive me," he said.

As I continued with preparing the children's meal, I started thinking about when a spouse has been tempted into adultery, you have to take so many things into consideration. *Is he standing in my face begging because he was caught? Is he sincere? Will this happen again? Is this the first time?* I needed answers. *Was this the beginning of a failing marriage or the path to rebuilding a strong relationship?* I must admit, I did not want to impulsively make a hasty decision.

After putting dinner in the oven, I joined Robert in the family room. We knew we had so much to lose. I put our wedding video on to see if this man really loved me when we got married or if he just wanted the security of a relationship. When our wedding song played, we both burst into tears. Robert sobbed. When you get married, you will see a lot of things unexpectedly. I did feel his sincerity, but my pain did not subside.

We reached a place at that moment where we could not even talk. We felt the loss and the pain. Besides, there was nothing he could say that would satisfy me at the time. I wanted to separate.

The children were still playing in the playroom. I called the children downstairs and sat them on the sofa.

"Dad and I have decided not to live together anymore." Our three and five-year-old were confused. My eight-year-old started talking about the children at school whose parents were separated.

"Mom," Lauren said, "I never thought this would happen to our family. Why are you and Daddy divorcing? So, does this mean Dad won't live in the same house?"

"Honey, sometimes people make poor decisions about rules. These decisions can affect everyone in their surroundings. I can't make you understand because you are just a little too young. But I will explain someday."

Lauren started to cry. It was very upsetting because she had never heard us talk about separating before.

"So, how will we see Dad every day? I don't know who I'm going to even live with! My friends at school always go to their father's house on Friday's. They have their suitcase when they come to school. Mom, please don't make us split up," she cried.

I allowed her to express her feelings. Kids know more than we think. After reaching over to hug her, Robert had to leave the room. He must have stormed out of the back door to go for a walk or something. To see my oldest baby burst into tears made the situation more complicated.

"Everything will work out somehow, Lauren," I said.

The younger two just continued to play.

I was very scared at this point. Why was life so complicated? Should I have been faced with a situation that I had no time to even contemplate? Although my emotions were ripped apart, I could not think about just my feelings. I had to consider what was best for the children also.

The children had gone off somewhere into the house again when Robert came back into the family room. "Karen, we can work this out. I promise I will spend a lifetime trying to make up for what has happened in our marriage."

"Robert, you know what? I have tried to be the best woman a man could ever desire, but somehow this was not good enough. Now, if you want to work through this, start by being honest. If you are even thinking about lying, our marriage is over even if the physical separation has not taken place. Who was this whore that you had sex with?"

"Why would you want to know that?" he asked.

"Oh, you can't tell the little secret? Okay. Hold on to all of the details to spare my feelings after they are splattered all over the place right now! I really just cannot believe you. You just don't want your marriage. And that's fine by me. If I'm going to hurt, I'd rather hurt now and get over it than listen to you continue to lie."

"I just don't want to make things worse!" he yelled.

"Look, the covenant is broken. It can only get worse if you're not honest with yourself or me. Robert, I want to know from the beginning to the end what happened. After all, if I'm in the grocery store, I could be right behind the woman who had intercourse with my saved man."

"This is crazy," he said.

"Why? Is it because you have to consciously make a decision whether

25

or not to lie and lose everything or tell the truth and still risk losing everything? So, which part of this is crazy?"

"Okay, Karen. I really didn't want to make matters worse." He started telling the story to me about who she was and how they met. I was so scared. I wanted to know, but part of me wanted him to just lie and say that all of this was just one bad dream.

"Is it someone that I know?"

"No, you don't know her, Karen. I met her at her office, and we talked about careers and really nothing else. I was working on the sales promotion package for the new product line."

I knew this was going to hurt, but every woman wants to know who could entice her husband to risk his life and marriage over sex.

"Karen, this is not an excuse, but she just told me how smart I was, and it seemed like I really had it going on."

I just sat and listened for a moment. Unjustified, he still had feelings also.

"So, before I knew it, she kissed me on my cheek, telling me to have a blessed day. I knew she wanted more, but I wasn't sure whether or not to push her away. Before I knew it, it got out of hand."

"What got out of hand?" I said calmly. I had to remember not to scream because I asked him for the details. Therefore, I did not want to attack him for giving them to me. He sat on the chair as if he really knew that this was the straw that broke the camel's back. In all reality, I think it was. I knew right away that God would have to make a miracle for me to get through this mess.

"Rob, these are the type of things that happen when you consider yourself as "innocently" flirting."

"We did something we both knew was wrong. We didn't fully undress, so when it was over, I washed and hauled out of the door. I could not believe how stupid I was to do that. When I drove off from her office, I didn't know what to do."

On edge, wondering if this woman could have gotten pregnant, I softly spoke, "Robert, did you leave your seed?"

"What do you mean, Karen?"

"Did you leave your sperm in that stranger?"
"No. I am so ashamed."

"I just want you to be honest right now," I said. "So, was she worth it?"

"No! And I know I'm in trouble with God. I did repent, but I still feel terrible."

I was too hurt to tell him that God's mercies are renewed every morning. At the time, I could not say that God's grace was sufficient. I was hurt. This was not quality living. I would rather hug an oversized pillow at night.

We sat quietly. The both of us were so sad. I mean really sad. It seemed as if we were two kids who got caught with our hands in the cookie jar waiting to hear the punishment. He started telling me her name and where she worked. The fact that I truly loved this man sitting in front of me made it very difficult for me to sit so patiently. I realized that, unlike some marriages, I was never looking for a way out of the relationship. The companionship was great, but obviously there was a serious communication breakdown. I just didn't understand how my saved man could cheat on me. There was so much good still in the marriage, yet there was excruciating pain from the betrayal.

There is a stigma in reference to saved men that they are almost perfect. Christian people are sinners being healed daily. Although I knew this, it was so hard to absorb.

"This would not affect me as much if I didn't love you so much," I said.

"Karen, I want you to know, me messing up had nothing to do with you."

"I know. This was your own dysfunction. I am not going to take the blame for you being unfaithful. Even if there were a problem in the marriage, you don't resolve it by having intercourse with another woman. Don't you think that is just adding fuel to the fire?"

"Regardless of what decision you make, I realize I may have destroyed my life. I know you are the most beautiful person a man could ever desire. You are everything I need and more. If I could take back the damage, I would do anything. I wish I could take all of that aching pain from your heart. I love you, no matter what happens," he said.

"For the sake of the children, I will at least try therapy and then make a sound decision," I responded.

Couples Therapy

We both sought a therapist who believed in the sanctity of marriage. Sometimes you may have to try a few before you find one who is suitable for your personality. Ironically, Robert never wanted counseling before. He knew there was a communication gap, but he felt he could handle this without help.

Somehow men automatically think women will immediately spank them on the hand and easily forget how they were betrayed. I had no intention of allowing this to calmly go up under the rug. I did know that if we could not be faithful to one another I wanted to end the relationship.

We had never been in counseling before. I made arrangements

to find a therapist we were both comfortable with. Our first appointment was very frightening. The thought of telling a stranger your personal business was unfamiliar territory for me and Robert. We met with Susan at a counseling center for marriages. I didn't know what type of questions to even ask when we interviewed her. She was a little feisty, but I thought I could overlook that. Susan was very rigid concerning infidelity. She told me that she could help me get through a divorce and direct me to all of the support I would need. I was so confused. I still did not know if the marriage should just be given up.

"Karen, I have a friend at the sandwich shop down the street that I could introduce you to. I mean, men can really be a challenge, and you sometimes have to keep moving until you find the right one."

"Susan, are you actually suggesting that I meet another man while I'm still married and trying to work through my relationship? First of all, even if I had decided to divorce, I wouldn't date someone during the grieving process. That would only confuse his life and my children. The last thing I need is a man to make me feel like I have overcome the breakup with Robert. Are you married, Susan?"

"No. I was, but my husband did the exact same thing to me. He left and remarried. But, I'm happy, Karen."

"That's good if that resolve works for you. Robert and I value our vows. We have a problem that needs to be worked through, but all marriages have problems. I have agreed to try to make it work. I don't think you can counsel us."

Without hesitation, I gave her the hourly check and told her to have a good day.

"Oh, by the way, this is my last visit," I said. "Thanks for everything."

"Karen, I'm sorry. I just know how painful adultery is, and I wanted you to know that if you wanted to leave, I could support your decision."

"I know. But I want to save the marriage like I said. Susan, maybe you need to deal with that hurt concerning the abandonment from your own husband. Thanks, again."

Although we had to look for another therapist, it was so vital that we found someone who would at least try to work with us through this. Susan was not the right one. We finally found an excellent person with whom our personalities were very comfortable.

The New Therapist

"Hello, how are you today?" Dr. Maria inquired.

Robert and I responded simultaneously, "Good."

"So, what is the situation in your marriage?"

"Adultery," I responded.

"Well, do you want to work through this or work toward separating?"

"We want our marriage to survive this," Robert said.

I asked Dr. Maria how she felt about marriage and the commitments. She merely explained all of the biblical principles in reference to marriage. "Now, I am married and do know that it takes both parties to really work on the relationship."

This is just what we needed to hear. Our first session with her felt good. When we went to the car, Robert and I agreed that she would be the one to help us through our crisis. She was a very level-headed individual and she had a warm, comforting personality.

During the sessions, many tears were shed, and situations came out that we had never even considered. Somehow I felt like I was processing this big mess. Sitting on Dr. Maria's neutral-colored, plush leather sofa, Robert and I shared a box of Kleenex. I wept.

"I just don't understand how this could have happened. We were so happy. Why didn't he tell me there was a void in our relationship? I feel like he didn't give me a chance. This isn't fair. Dr. Maria, Robert made a vow to God and to me."

The therapist said, "You can make it through this if you are willing to do the work. Robert, are you willing to make this work?" she asked.

"Yes," he responded. "I told my wife I would do whatever it takes to keep our marriage and family together."

"Alright. I will need to see the both of you every week for about an hour until you feel more comfortable in the relationship."

"Dr. Maria, when will we see progression?" I asked.

"That depends on the couple. Some marriages overcome within a year, and some take much longer. Remember, this is a process. Don't expect a quick fix. Okay, guys, put up a good fight for your marriage. I have worked with so many families, and they've won the war."

A few weeks passed. Going to the family church, I started to feel so artificial. I walked into the sanctuary with a deep, heart-filled sorrow. No one there knew what was going on, not even the pastor. Besides, I could never tell anyone in my church. Robert was so highly respected. We had our image to uphold...isn't that ironic? Robert chose to sit with our family for a few Sundays as he decided to get things aligned at home before actively volunteering in the church again. Luckily, the church had a large membership, and had other helpers. I didn't want him to sit down after confessing everything to me. After all, I was willing to forgive. I just couldn't do it at that time. I did feel bad that I couldn't forgive so easily.

Service ended, and everyone greeted each other. "Praise the

Lord, Sis!" A prophet said as she approached me through the thickness of the crowd. "God wants me to tell you that your husband may be putting you through hell, but you are going to come out smelling like a bed of roses!" She delivered her message and walked away.

God is so amazing, I said to myself. I looked around to see if anyone had seen her talking to me. Everyone was walking out of the church or talking and laughing with each other. I did not know this prophet's name, nor did she know mine. I guess that's irrelevant when God wants to send an encouraging word. It was shocking because she knew nothing about me or my personal life.

God is omnipotent. Many times, we are looking for Him to use the preacher to give us a word, but when we least expect it, He shows up in a different way—a way that is totally unfamiliar. I mean, this prophet walked away as if she had never said a word to me. I honestly could not believe those words that ran off of her tongue. To explain how miraculous it really was, God used a total stranger. She was not friends with anyone I knew or hung around. She left me standing there in a state of shock. The Lord loves us so much He sends voices from the angels to encourage our walk with Him. He wanted me to be aware that regardless of how it may look, He would never leave or forsake me.

CHAPTER THREE

If You See My Husband, Would You Please Send Him Home?

I t was weeks after the betrayal, but I still felt like I still needed much self care and time alone. I woke up on another Sunday morning and decided to go to church by myself. I felt really good about how I was progressing through therapy, and I was beginning to feel like myself again. When I went to church, I was very emotional during worship service. Truly the Spirit of God was consoling my heart. Then the pastor walked to the podium and started preaching a message that was so encouraging. It was as if he knew every issue I was dealing with. I felt empowered. After hearing his words, I knew I could get through my challenges. The power of the Word of God seemed like music in my ears; so inspiring yet comforting.

After the church service was over, as I was driving home I continued to meditate on the steps I felt I needed to take to give me some sort of ease about what Robert had shared with me. Remembering Robert's confession of who he cheated with, I had the urge to speak with that woman. I was not in a rage or angry. I just wanted to know the truth. I stopped by the office building where Robert told me she worked. Not sure if anyone would be there, I entered the building. A young receptionist opened the door to let me in as she greeted me.

"Good morning. Is Tracey here today?" I asked pleasantly.

"No, I'm afraid she's off today," she responded.

"She'll be here tomorrow. Can I give her a message? What is this in regards to, because I can call her at home if it's important?"

"Well, it's sort of personal."

"Let me try to get her at home," she said. "Hi, Tracey. There's a young lady here to see you."

The receptionist passed the phone to me. "Hello, Tracey. My name is Karen. Is it possible for you to meet somewhere today? I just want to talk alone."

"Okay," Tracey said. "You're not going to hurt me or anything?"

"No, I just want to talk. Let's meet about five minutes away from your office building at the Center Plaza," I responded.

I could not believe this was happening. I was going to meet the person who shared my bedroom goodies. Dressed very refined as usual, I was ready to confront her. The plan was not to attack her because Robert was definitely equally wrong. I just wanted to find out why she had to have sex with my husband when she knew he was married.

While waiting patiently, a little boxed car pulled up beside my black 740 BMW. I got out to greet her. Noticing she had her son in the back seat, I wondered if she were married. Her son looked like he was about five years old.

She walked over to meet me, and I noticed that I really didn't have too much competition. As a matter of fact, I wasn't willing to compete. If someone wants you in their life, it's up them to appreciate who they are in a relationship with.

How could this woman possibly cause my husband to fall? I mean, she wasn't bad looking. She just wasn't as pretty as I. Her hair was not pinned or even in a neat bun. Her skin was not as flawless as mine. In other words, she must have had a strong conversation to entice my man. Anyways, he fell for her, and I would definitely get to the end of the whole story.

"Hi, my name is Karen Butler and my husband, Robert, met with you a couple of months ago regarding some new products on the market."

"Oh, I remember Robert. What does this have to do with me?"

"My husband said the two of you had sex at your office."

"Oh, my God! He told you? Why would he tell you something like that? Believe me, Karen. I went through adultery before with my husband, and we were separated for almost two years. I can't believe he told you."

"Karen, that is very painful to go through, and I could never do that to my worst enemy. I just wanted to let you know that if he has admitted to having sex with you. It wasn't with me."

"Tracey, why would he tell me all of your information if it were just one big lie? He said you guys had a quickie in the office."

"I can't believe he told you," she repeatedly said.

"Did you have sex with Robert?"

"No," she said as if she were in disbelief that I confronted her. "Robert and I had a long conversation about the products he was selling and our careers. That's as far as it went."

This woman was not innocent, and I knew it in my spirit.

"As a matter of fact, Robert discussed with me that he was married with children, and you guys had a great business in the southern part of the city. He wanted to play, but I didn't Karen."

"Did you kiss him on the cheek?"

"Just a little innocent peck."

"How was it innocent if he is a married man? Why did you kiss him anyway?" I really wanted to slap her across the face, but the love of God would not allow me to stoop that low. Besides, that could be a soul that needed to be saved. "Tracey, aren't you faithfully married? If you were only talking about business, how did you get to the state of kissing him on his face?"

"Okay, he wanted to pursue me, but I didn't."

"Whatever!" I said. "Did he have his wedding band on?"

"Yes. I knew he was married. But, Karen, I'm married, and again there was unfaithfulness in my marriage."

"Tracey, with your experience in an adulterous relationship, I'm sure you know how hurtful it can be to the offended survivor. Do you realize people get killed over stupidity such as this? That was someone's husband. Do me a favor; if you ever have the opportunity with someone else's man, if you see our husbands, would you please send them home?"

"Karen, I'm so sorry this happened to you," she said while she held her hand on my shoulder.

"Please don't touch me. I want to thank you for meeting with me. If you don't think about anyone else, think about how you have contributed to destroying a family with young children. Why? For nothing more than selfishness."

I left her standing there puzzled. She seemed as if she wanted to come clean and confess to the offense but didn't know how I would respond. Either way, it didn't matter. I knew she was the person. Everything added up that Robert had shared with me, although I was still so upset that he did this to me.

I felt free because I had confronted Satan and actually called him out. There was such an energy that arose within me. I didn't feel so helpless. I drove home talking to myself. I couldn't believe she met with me. I really was glad about that. So now when I was in the grocery store, I would at least know who that individual was. Although I may never know if there were others, at least I was able to quench my curiosity.

Many women do know that these irresponsible men are married. Pushing mid-life, they sometimes just want to see if they still have it. Often, they are playing with the idea of an opportunity not thinking of possible tragedies that will take place. Whatever the reason, it's all sin. I do place emphasis on the fact that it is sin.

Undercover Relationships

A government agency that I worked for was a campout for undercover relationships. My co-worker Tabitha dated a married man. I asked her if he was married, and she said, "Yeah, but maybe he'll leave his wife and two kids."

"Isn't this smart? Throwing a challenge out there, hoping a man will leave his family but cleave to you. What do you imagine would happen to your relationship if he did leave his wife? Anyhow, Tibby," I said, "I don't want to get in your business, but this man has only been married for three years. Why interfere with his marriage?"

"Well, if he is dumb enough to play, I don't have anybody, so it's better than being alone. I don't know," she said. "I'm just going to enjoy it while it lasts."

Some time had passed on when Tibby miraculously became pregnant. Now she's still without the man of her dreams. But the child does have a father living in an already-made household. Can you imagine when parent-teacher conferences are held? That dad has to be active in a couple of different schools. This is just crazy. We need to stop thinking selfishly about what we need and think about our children, who are the future leaders.

A couple of Robert's business associates had a horrible situation. Brandon and Trina got married without even attempting to get marriage counseling. Robert asked Brandon, "Are you really going to marry that girl?"

"Yes, I am. I would be crazy not to have those beautiful legs."

"Okay, man, marriage can be challenging," Robert said. "I surely hope you know what you're doing."

The courthouse wedding was sudden. After about two years, Brandon grew bored with Trina's legs. He wanted to try someone different, so he ended up having an affair. Brandon eventually left his wife and children for a playmate. He was going to church quite often and professing to be saved, but he got caught up in the moment. His decision to move out of his home with another woman left major bitterness with his wife. I think this is what they call a mid-life crisis. After being out there for a while, he begged his wife's forgiveness and asked to move back into their home.

This was another perfect example for the other woman to encourage that man to go back to his wife. Well, anyway, after he moved back, Trina became vindictive and wanted to file for a divorce. She told him there was nothing to work out.

Brandon told Trina he was sorry for abandoning the family. Trina said it was a little too late. She had a friend in the new church she was attending, and he was very interested in establishing a permanent relationship.While Brandon was telling us about his dilemma, he explained that the boyfriend was supposed to be a God-chaser. She divorced him Brandon Of course, she had that option due to his infidelity.

The True State of Christian Marriages

Sadly, this is happening far too often in our churches. I may not be able to change the world's way of handling relationships, but if I could just prevent a few marriages from going down the nightmare stream of adultery, my mission will be done.

Oftentimes you want couples to stay together and tough it out like our parents did, but when dealing with infidelity, there is such a huge invasion on your territory that you feel it is almost impossible to survive. After your spouse has been with another woman, something dies within you. Therefore, it takes two people to make the decision to save the marriage. Just realize that eighty percent of the marriages that decide to stay and work it out do actually grow.

Talking to various couples, some people give up immediately on the relationship by going right out and having an affair also. This is like throwing gasoline on an open flame. Why? Although what happened was not fair, you should not start a relationship with another man. It really complicates the healing process. You would also be taking all of that hurt into another relationship.

I was vacationing in one of the Caribbean islands one summer. There was a nice bonfire going and it was very romantic. My husband and I stood around talking to the other couples at the resort. One guy approached me discreetly, asking me for sex. He said to me, "Come on, you're in the Bahamas. No one back home will ever know what you do here."

I just smiled and walked back over to my husband. That's a slogan that's used quite a bit. When you're away, no one will ever know what you've done. Trust me. The devil is lying to Christians every day about how they can get away with sin. Take Adam and Eve and their story in Genesis. When God forbade them to eat of a particular tree, Eve allowed Satan to persuade her. Satan told her that they would become little gods. He lied to her. Always know that what the enemy tells you that the Bible does not support, it is meant to destroy you.

God goes on vacation with us. He goes to work with us. Everywhere we are, He is. He chose us to live a sacrificial life. We serve Him out of the love and appreciation we have for the bloodshed through Christ.

CHAPTER FOUR

The Cracker Jack Prize

I have a comparison to marriages as Cracker Jack boxes. Cracker Jacks are the sweet favorites of many people. Not only does the sweet buttery toffee hit that sweet tooth, but there is also a little prize in each box! Robert and I would always share a bag. You have no idea what the prize is going to be, but you enjoy that sticky popcorn with the sweet peanuts. We would just sit, munch, and talk. It's one of our most memorable moments. I sometimes say, "I wonder what the little prize is going to be." I usually have no idea.

This concept is comparable to marriages. I know you're asking, "How would a sticky little snack have anything to do with a covenant between two people?" Let me explain. When you first get married, you're flowing in the popcorn. Life's so great. You finally got what you've waited for. You may see some small flaws, but nothing major. Anyway, you feel you can endure anything that may challenge that bond. No one can come between the two of you. Your lovely husband can say nothing wrong. Even if he offends someone, you apologize for him. As time passes on, you eventually get that little prize. When it's exposed, you wonder how this surprise could be in that package. It's not what you expected. You begin to become aware of the fact that you don't want it, and you can't send it back. Do you stop eating

41

that snack out of frustration? Or, do you just throw the whole package away? There is always a choice.

There's no possible way to know everything there is to know about your spouse before you marry. You can spend as much time together as possible, but as you grow, different situations may arise. Some problems are great, but it does not mean they can't be worked through. You have a choice. Don't feel hopeless. Count the positives in the marriage before you give up and file for divorce. Do you have any good in that relationship? I know hurt can overtake decision making but fight to save what God has blessed you with. Then, if it is not salvageable, consider making a decision. We should not stay in an adulterous relationship if it's a matter of life or death.

When I had to go through that infidelity in my marriage, I found that there was no one to really talk to. First of all, I know women are trying to cover their homes and keep those secrets. But what do you do when your spouse is saved and has fallen? Where do you go? Who can you talk to? The pressure was unbearable. I think that we are more critical of this and many other problems in a marriage due to the biblical principles. These principles are great because they give standards to live by, but we are not perfected overnight. We must grow to that level of perfection. We can't look at our mate and immediately give up on him. God definitely can change him. Notice I said, "God." There is no way we can nag faithfulness into them. But when God does it, He reaches areas that we could never go. Marriage is not all popcorn without a prize.

I remember going to my twentieth-class reunion. It was shocking to see a couple of the most popular and likely to succeed classmates on drugs or who had experienced an unimaginable fall in their lives. Life can bring so much joy, yet pain as well. What I have learned is to embrace all areas of life's challenges and never judge. That one situation that we may judge, or fear is what we may have to experience.

Amazingly, the one person you love so much can do no wrong. Even though you know he's not perfect, subconsciously you think he's actually flawless. I never liked surprises, such as birthday parties, showers, or getaways. I always wanted to know what to expect. If you're not going to get any surprises, then you can pass through this journey of life very comfortably. If someone told you that the one you love was going to be sexually active with another person, you would immediately make an impulsive decision to vacate. This does sound logical, because you don't know what is in the future.

After being married for so many years, I have learned that in all relationships there is at least one little skeleton in the closet. We know that skeletons are dry bones in the valley. The Bible is the most profound book in the world. In this book, Ezekiel 37 speaks of dry bones in the valley. But God says he will put flesh on them and connect bone to bone. I believe this is the beginning of repentance and a new walk with God.

We were all born in sin and shaped in iniquity. Without repentance, nothing good can come out of sin. It's funny how we look at other people and judge them because we don't have the same weaknesses. But if we look at ourselves long enough, we will find distasteful characteristics that we wouldn't want revealed.

The prize in the Cracker Jack box is so small to a God who is so great. Just have an open and willing heart to change. Then allow God to do the work. Remember to have patience. These changes are a process. Nothing is perfected overnight. We strive for perfection.

CHAPTER FIVE

Permission To Grieve

Accepting the truth that my husband had cheated was a very difficult process. I honestly didn't know how to handle things or what to feel. My reality was that the man I loved had betrayed my love and my trust. I must have processed this reality thousands of times in my head. It took such a toll on me mentally, spiritually, and physically. For days, I only showered and put sweatpants on. I didn't want to put on makeup or doll myself up, there was no eyeliner, lipstick, or blush. I was hurt, and I didn't care what I looked like on the outside. I just couldn't get myself to be motivated again.

I stopped smiling and laughing with my family and friends. I saw people, but they didn't look real. I heard them speak, but the voices were fading away. I had no control over what was happening to me. Everything seemed like one big, hard bubble. I thought people around me had changed tremendously, but in all reality, I was changing. I couldn't trust anyone. I even started to question God. How could He allow the man He told me to marry to betray me? Some things that our Father does just don't make sense to tiny minds. I was hurt, and I didn't know what to do with it.

When we started therapy, I asked the counselor if there was a prescription or something that could ease the pain because I physically felt this in my body. The stress was unbearable. The counselor told me to allow the healing process to work at its own pace. Then I realized that I had to feel every ounce of that pain. I fell to my knees and asked God to be with me.

One of the struggles I had was the continuous thought "what if he commits adultery again?" I definitely had to consider that question. I was vulnerable knowing there could be a possibility that this could happen again. The more time elapsed I realized that I needed to grieve what happened. I had to grieve the hurt and the betrayal and how it made me feel. I thought I had to be so strong, but the pain was tearing me apart. Holding my head up, and trying to stay stable was tough. The truth is, I first had to be restored, because trying to walk through the confusion of my world that had crumbled made it impossible for me to focus. I felt like I had been escorted out into the deep of the ocean and was let go. As hard as I tried to act normal, it just was not happening. You may understand how sometimes there are obstacles surrounding you when you're trying to get somewhere, but you just can't seem to make them disappear.

I wondered, where do I begin to get back on my feet? Emotionally, I wanted to be the same so badly, but I couldn't. I wanted my marriage to be normal, but it wasn't. Some circumstances completely bring you to a halt and make you re-evaluate the quality of life you're living.

Keeping my Christian values, I had a difficult time giving myself permission to grieve. After all, this was not supposed to happen to me. I never did anything intentionally to hurt anyone. So why would this betrayal stop at my front door?

I could not see how God could possibly get any glory out of my pain. I must have cried for about two weeks. The pain just would not subside. I had to heal this wound and restore the peace in my mind. In the old small churches, the old folks used to say, "He's a mind regulator." I never knew what they were talking about because I was too young. But I truly needed God to regulate my thought patterns and my mind.

Where is God?

Does He feel the pain I feel?

Doesn't He see the open humiliation and shame that I am going through?

If God loves me, why would he allow me to be openly embarrassed by people I had witnessed to about Him?

Despite all of the questions, I had to trust God that everything would work out for my good. My feelings were flying everywhere. And no, they weren't holy either! I was so angry and frustrated. I was not ready to end this marriage. But in reality, it felt like it ended when he decided to cheat. It amazes me how people think that if your man had a one-night stand it's okay. But, if he had an ongoing affair, then that's worse. All of it breaks the covenant between you, God, and the spouse. Betrayal is betrayal. You never know the real truth about someone who has betrayed you and been caught.

Grieving the Loss

"Although not all partners hurt by an affair will develop post-traumatic stress disorder (PTSD) reactions, many will experience grief and depression. Hurt partners may become obsessed with the affair's details, feel powerless with their emotions, and need therapeutic assistance at such times."[2]

As I attempted to go through my healing process, I realized that I needed to give myself permission to grieve. Merriam-Webster

---

[2] Jinashree Rajendrakumar, "The Grief of an Affair (Your partner cheated. Now what? Part 2)," South Tampa Therapy Blog, August 17th, 2021, https://southtampacounselor.com/blog/tag/Marriage+Therapy, (accessed 12/5/21)

dictionary identifies Grief as "a cause of deep sadness."[3] When you encounter this type of pain you may not know how to grieve. This was something I had to learn how to do. The truth is your grieving process is a personal experience.

We must be careful when handling crises to properly grieve and allow God to heal the pain. If we're not careful Satan will try to introduce us to substances that would bring harm to our bodies like drugs or alcohol, with the lies that it will help ease the pain. Although it may seem to temporarily allow you to escape, you will still need to face the pain head on, once you come down from the false high. Whatever your weakness was before you committed your life to Christ, Satan will tempt you to go back to it. So, not only do you fight temptation, you are dealing with the hurt also. But if you stay in God's house and adhere to the word of God, He will never fail.

My advice to anyone experiencing this is to allow yourself to grieve the great loss. Regardless of the position you hold in your career or church, allow yourself to grieve at your own pace. Don't try to pretend you are healed right away because you are used to being a strong person with great leadership skills. I actually consider the grief period as couch time. Everybody needs it at some time or another. While you are healing you must be okay with not being okay.

As you are going through your process you may feel lonely and that you don't have much support from your friends and family. Society is more supportive of someone who lost a spouse in the case of death. They show their support by bringing food to your home and constantly calling to see if there is anything they can do to help. Therefore, when people around you know that you're experiencing an emotional death, don't try to respond as if nothing traumatic has happened in your life. Although crying is healthy, you do not have to

---

[3] "Grief," Merriam-Webster, https://www.merriam-webster.com/dictionary/grief, (accessed 12/5/21)

constantly cry on your best friend's shoulder but allow them to understand that there has been a death in your life.

You are Not Alone

Facing the imperfections of marriage is healthy. Don't look at couples around you and compare yourself to them. Many people put their happy faces on when in public. This is why you hear of marriages ending in divorce after twenty years. The normal response is, "I thought they were so happy." We have many actresses and actors in the world, but many stories change behind closed doors. There is no perfect relationship. I had to understand that even the holiest, perfect, best-dressed, well-to-do families struggle with infidelity. You are never alone. Someone may even say to you, "I would never stay in my marriage if adultery was ever the case." They never know what they would do if they went through unfaithfulness. Besides, we must be so careful lest our mouths condemn us. No, we may not have any intention of becoming trapped, but if we live long enough, life can put us in places we never had intentions of going to. It's God's grace that preserves our souls. I am grateful for His mercies.

Don't Place Blame on Others

I also had to careful not to blame anyone for my husband's infidelity. It would be wrong of me accuse others around me as if they knew about the infidelity and chose not to tell me. People do not want to involve themselves with private matters that they cannot prove and honestly that right. However, while you are hurt you will be vulnerable but try to focus on your marriage and not what you feel others around you should say or do.

Slow Down and Heal

While I was going through my struggles, I had to be very patient with my healing process. As I was working on my emotional healing, I decided to take some much needed self-care time. I spent some time away at a resort in West Virginia. I guess you would call this my couch time. I really did need it. My head was so cluttered. It was as if I woke up one morning and had a family and didn't know what to do with them. So yes, I was scared. Life doesn't stop for anyone. Everything just kept moving, business as usual but I needed a break from it all.

When I arrived to the resort, they assigned me to my own cabin. Very interestingly, I forgot that it was a health awareness center and I wanted some junk food. There was no radio, television, or fireplace. Could I survive a few days without these luxuries? Immediately, I turned my cell phone off and knelt to pray.

"Lord, please help me to make a good decision. You know Robert better than I. Only you know what the future holds concerning our marriage. I am hurt, and I don't want to impulsively decide out of anger."

With weeping tears, I fell off into a deep, peaceful sleep.

Going through your healing process is a requirement. It may seem at times that you won't be able to make it through. You'll want to stay in a dark room and feel sorry for yourself. But guess what? You'll make it through those times no matter how hard it gets. God has placed His purpose inside of you and this is not the end of your story, trust me you can get through this.

Healing is a process and below are five (5) steps I consider to be important to recognize and assess during your recovery time.

1. **Admit to the Infidelity** - Don't be in denial or naïve to the offense.

Accept what has happened. Remember, the most beautiful, richest, famed, articulate women get betrayed by adultery. Yes, this sin has occurred and it's hard work to get through the healing process. Think of it this way. Let's say you got an extremely deep cut to your arm and needed stitches. What would be the first step you would take to heal? I'm sure you would go to an emergency room, right? Why? You need medical attention. The on-call doctor would first see how deep the cut is. Do you need stitches or even surgery?

The trauma we go through varies among individuals. But we first need to be assessed, even if our mate doesn't feel the need to. Our emotions are the same. The difference is we have internal bleeding that no one can see. We scream for salvation from a toxic relationship, but no sound comes out. Your hurt is there, and it is real. It shows up in every aspect of your life: through other relationships, business, jobs, etc. Admit to the pain and shun the guilt, embarrassment, and shame.

2. **Grieve - There are five (5) stages to grief.**

a. **Stage 1:** Denial - sort of numb to what's going on. Denial is the first stage of grief. During my grieving I had to acknowledge that I had never felt like that before, and I could no longer lie to myself that everything was all right, because it wasn't. I could not deny what happened or how it affected me. I could not deny that I had totally fallen apart inside. I could not eat or sleep! Before this happened, I thought I had my life together. Any trial that would come my way, I knew it wouldn't knock me out. Boy was I wrong, and I couldn't deny that this was so much more than I could handle.

As I started thinking carefully, it was possible that I saw signs but ignored them. After all, Robert was never interested in sharing our bedroom goodies with another woman. How could I have lied to myself? I now had to accept where I was in life and deal with it. I'm not saying I had to allow a man to disrespect me, but I had to make a destiny decision in reference to whom I had married.

b. **Stage 2:** Bargaining - Maybe this is my fault. To alleviate admitting that he has betrayed you, you think of ways you contributed to his infidelity. Remember he made a decision to step out of the relationship.

c. **Stage 3**: Depression - Realizing I have been betrayed. I thought he truly loved me. Depression-reality sets in. You may get really sad and don't feel like doing your normal activities. This is okay temporarily. If it persists, seek medical attention. Connect with a good friend; someone you can trust.

d. **Stage 4:** Anger - Feeling outright helpless. To build a few years with someone who betrays you can make you extremely angry. If you can take a couple days away to prevent getting physical, do this. You may think I don't deserve this. You may feel betrayed by God also. How could God let this happen? I've been faithful to the church, and various ministries. Again, understand man has the power to choose right or wrong.

e. **Stage 5:** Acceptance - Acknowledge and accept that infidelity has happened. Know that you can choose to stay or leave. Before deciding, pray and ask God for his direction.

3. **Reunite and Seek Therapy -** If you decide to continue in the marriage, understand your path has shifted majorly. Rededicate your vows to one another. Now that you both see how easy it is to separate, you should have a different view on how fragile a marriage can be. Close in tight. Put the children to bed. Turn the cell phones off. Rotate listening and talking every 15 minutes without interrupting the person who's speaking. It's time to reunite on purpose. Make the decision to grow from the betrayal.

4. **Re-construct -** Communication is the main ingredient to a successful marriage. Take foundational steps to rebuild the

marriage. Have accountability to your spouse. List reasons why you want to stay in the marriage, and the pros and cons. Some things may need to be removed or added to strengthen the relationship.

5. **Share** - Be a support to help others with their processes. As God salvages your marriage and grace you to endure such a devastating pivotal time in your life, reach back and help someone else who has nowhere to turn.

As you work through your grief process, please minimize your home and work responsibilities and if possible, invest more in your self-care and journaling. Ask God to guide you through your decision making; to separate or stay. Have lunch with a close friend, seek individual therapy, take a couple of days to a retreat alone, etc. Allow yourself to grieve such a great loss. Remember, even if you decide to continue in the marriage, you have lost trust and been betrayed. Don't continue to build on broken pieces, it eventually will collapse. Sit with your feelings and don't let anyone try to confuse you on how you should feel. Listen to your heart. It never lies. Your future is brighter whether you decide to stay or disconnect with your husband. God our Father "will never leave you nor forsake you" (Hebrews 13:5 KJV). He will always send you the support you need to get through tough times.

CHAPTER SIX

Choosing to Forgive

I have seen women walk around angry with their spouses for years and never confront what has taken place. I didn't want to become a bitter little lady. Although I had so much to risk by putting my business on hold for expansion, I knew I needed to deal with what was going on at home and face it head on. I could not brush this up under the rug and spank him on the hand, trying to pretend nothing ever happened. I truly feel that if these situations are dealt with early on, it's possible to stop them from reoccurring through outside professional help. Also, I believe that if it's ignored, your mate will continue to play. Understand that some people are not willing to surrender after an affair. You must pray and decide whether or not to hang in there.

Most of the time when infidelity has invaded the relationship, other emotional issues come up with the victim. I guess you can call it Pandora's Box. Once it's opened, everything in it has to be addressed. I gave myself permission to mourn the loss of innocence in the relationship and it took admitting that something had gone wrong. It was possible that I also played a role in the pitfall. I'm not saying that I caused this unacceptable behavior, but I did share part of the communication breakdown. Yes, we think that when bad things happen, it's only because of our mate's dysfunction. Problems are a two-way street. Sometimes the core of the problem could come from the husband's or wife's upbringing. This is why I encourage counseling. But your spouse must first admit that there is a problem. If he never acknowledges the problem, then it will be difficult to get him to go to therapy or seek help. If your mate is being difficult or stubborn, ask God to intervene. God opens minds to allow people to see and acknowledge what they couldn't before.

Stop for a minute and ask God to reveal to you what should be uncovered and dealt with. He has a way of doing things without you having to do much to get to the bottom of what's really happening. To forgive you must deal with the root of the problem. But when you work on getting into the root of the problem, remember you are also taking risks. Keep in mind damage has occurred to your emotions, both spiritually and physically. Because it takes two to make your commitment work, I recommend going to a reputable family therapist, one who has a track record of marriage recovery.

During my reflections about the affair, I realized that my life at that time was so noisy; I couldn't hear anything. The relationship had started losing structure. We were still talking, but not about where his mind was or even the pressure I was under as my business was growing faster than I had anticipated. We were totally disconnected emotionally. I did not realize that until it was too late.

I want you to be truthful with yourself about where you are in the grief process. Be patient with yourself as you work through understanding where your relationship is today. The path that you thought was so good had serious flaws, but now that the issue has come forward, you can start a new journey and have a wholesome relationship if you decide to stay.

Forgiving Him

It is vital to go through the proper grieving process in order to forgive. Don't get confused with forgiving and denial. There is a major difference. As mentioned before, denial is the acceptance of what is going on in the relationship by making excuses. Oftentimes women will even accuse themselves of their spouse's unfaithful actions. Forgiveness is accepting and releasing. Let's take a closer look at this powerful characteristic.

Forgiving is a choice that can change the rest of your life. After grieving, which was a part of acceptance, I started choosing to forgive. This is one of the most difficult positions you may find yourself in. Forgiveness is always easy when you haven't been so connected to the person who offended you. It's different with a spouse.

Because of the impact of betrayal, trust is always a serious issue. There are some things we will go through that will make us doubt whether we have what it takes to forgive. The destruction is so great, almost like a cancerous tumor eating through the body. Forgiveness for me was a conscious effort. Every morning when I rose out of bed, I had to decide whether or not I wanted to feel the spirit of freedom or hold my husband captive. In an adulterous affair, we have a choice to leave or stay. If you make the choice to stay, don't hold on to past hurts. If the relationship is worth fighting for, it may be more difficult to look at your spouse every day and think about forgiving them as if you were the person who had intercourse outside of the relationship, but you can do it. Forgiveness takes the love of the Holy Spirit. I must confess that my heart wanted to forgive, but my mind needed more justification as to why the man I loved would even think about having an affair.

When we forgive the unfairness that has contaminated our lives, we release so much stress that can cause all types of bodily malfunctions. It takes energy to daily remember what someone has done to us. Can you imagine what accomplishments you could achieve with that negative energy? Yes, it takes much effort to remember how Satan is trying to destroy your life. Every morning when you wake up, thank God for forgiving you of your sins and ask him to help you to forgive others. It may be difficult because you don't think others deserve to be forgiven. But how is it that you think you deserve it? God's grace is still sufficient. Every day that you wake up is another opportunity to forgive.

Although I chose to forgive and eventually trust Robert, again, one of my most prominent struggles was trying to forgive him with the continuous thought "what if he commits adultery again?" Obviously, I had to consider asking myself that question. I was vulnerable knowing there could be a possibility that this could happen again if I chose to stay. The thought I had was only God knows the plan of the future.

What Does it Mean to Forgive?

To forgive means "to stop feeling angry or resentful toward (someone) for an offense, flaw, or mistake"[4] as defined by the Merriam-Webster dictionary. In contrast, trust means "to have a firm belief in the character, strength, or truth of someone or something"[5] referenced by Oxford languages. I learned how to forgive Robert first and then I learned how to trust him. Take a deep breath. We do not have to forgive and trust simultaneously.

The Word of God created a foundation for me to draw from. Matthew 6:14 KJV reads, "For if ye forgive men their trespasses, your Heavenly Father will also forgive you." The thought of forgiving was impossible to me in the beginning. My husband had committed the unforgivable sin. I never had to experience forgiveness to that depth. Forgiving was outright hard. Even before contemplating to forgive, it was difficult to hear what the Word of God says about

---

[4] "Forgive Definition & Meaning," Merriam-Webster, https://www.merriam-webster.com/dictionary/forgive, (accessed 12/18/21)

[5] "Trust Meaning & Definition for UK English," Lexico, Oxford, https://www.lexico.com/definition/trust, (accessed 12/18/21)

forgiving. I asked Robert, "What makes you think forgiving is an option although you asked for forgiveness?"

After realizing this would be a long road to recovery, I decided to forgive, although the manifestation had not taken place. In my mind I kept thinking what if I were in Robert's position asking for forgiveness? Conversely, I would definitely want him to forgive me. It took a couple of years at least before I felt the wounds had healed, I had fully forgiven him. I had to ask God consistently to help me. Occasionally there were questionable circumstances that would arise. Robert and I would sit and communicate through those concerns until I was comfortable.

Phases of Forgiveness

There were a few phases in me learning how to forgive that I want to share with you. First, I had to get over the anger because I didn't think he should be forgiven. I didn't judge or condemn myself for not being able to easily forgive him at the time because that was a natural emotion under those circumstances.

Listed below are five (5) phases to forgiveness that will help you with the process. These phases were very fruitful for my progression.

- **Phase 1.** Pair with the betrayal - Admitting/Acceptance is the prerequisite to forgiveness.

- **Phase 2.** Decision -You may have to repeat this step daily until you feel the manifestation. Keep in mind you must forgive whether or not you choose to stay in the marriage. Mark 11:24-25 KJV says, "Therefore, I say unto you, what things sever ye desire, when ye pray, believe that ye receive them, and ye shall have them. And when ye stand praying forgive, if ye have ought against any: that your Father also which is in heaven may forgive you your trespasses."

- **Phase 3.** Grace - an undeserving act: unmerited divine assistance given to man for their spiritual renewal or sanctification. 2 Corinthians 12:9 KJV, "And he said unto me, my grace is sufficient for thee: for my strength is made perfect in weakness. Most gladly therefore will I rather glory in my infirmities, that the power of Christ may rest upon me." During this grace period, be careful not to manipulate the marriage because he has violated the marriage vows."

- **Phase 4.** Don't be judgmental - It's very tempting to judge your spouse. Judging can cause retribution, whereas assessing the situation allows you to make a healthy plan of action to leave or stay. Of course, there are some inadequacies within the marriage, but allow him to seek the help he needs without you making him feel hopeless.

- **Phase 5.** Forget - You should not continuously bring the betrayal up after your relationship has advanced to a healthier level.

Be gentle with yourself because it does take a measure of time to process the thought of forgiving. Again, you are very emotional in which your thought pattern may change daily in the beginning. Understand that if you decide to separate from your marriage this does not mean you lack forgiveness. Perhaps, you may feel that you cannot forgive. That's okay. In due time I would hope you would eventually forgive your spouse in order to be free to live a purposeful, thriving life that you were destined to live.

Here are some questions I would like for you to consider in order to understand where you may be in the process. Now that I have shared a pathway to forgiveness, do you feel you can forgive your spouse?

1. Do you have the desire to get couples' / individual therapy and move forward with your life together? Remember no relationship is the same. Couples have various reasons why they feel a need to be unfaithful.
2. Do you feel he has sincerely repented?

3. Is he willing to re-establish the relationship with a true understanding that he must be guided by the Spirit of God?
4. Are you willing to be patient with the processes that God will develop him through?
5. Rebuilding is a small change daily. Do you think this hard work ahead will develop in a few months or years?
6. Can you continue to trust God although you're faced with this calamity?
7. Will you be in it to win it?
8. Did he own his unfaithfulness?
9. Can you ever be intimate with him, or would you rather refrain for a long period of time?
10. Are you willing to meet him where he is presently until he's pruned by God?

Don't be dismayed. You may be able to answer yes to some of these questions right now, but not all; this is not a test. There are transitional thoughts to scope the possibilities of being able to forgive.

CHAPTER SEVEN

When Trust is Broken

Once you make a decision to forgive, trust will need to be reestablished in your relationship. Forgiveness and trust are not the same thing.bI was reading an article that said, "forgiveness is given freely while trust has to be earned."[6] This couldn't be a truer statement. We can't talk about the issues in a broken relationship without dealing with the area of trust.

After I agreed to forgive my husband, we had to overcome the trust issue. Trusting my husband was almost impossible for me. It's important that I be transparent with you about this process because although it's necessary, it isn't easy. I became an undercover private investigator during the first few months after he cheated. I would look through his pockets and cell phone checking for phone numbers, phone log, business cards, receipts or anything that looked suspicious. I knew how long his travel commute to work should be, so I would clock the time of travel to and from work. I even checked his pay stubs to verify if there was unjustified leave.

Was this the first time he cheated?

Was his unfaithfulness ongoing?

How would I know whether or not he was telling me the truth?

These were questions I would ask myself. I thought I was losing my mind. I knew that in order to trust him, I had to be willing and able to forgive him. Without the Holy Spirit's help there was no way I could forgive or trust a man who had betrayed me. I did not trust him

---

[6] "Forgiveness is Free, Trust is Earned," Refine Us, http://refineus.org/forgiveness-vs-trust/, (accessed 12/18/21)

for a very long time. There was always some type of doubt in my mind whether or not he would do it again. Eventually, I had to release and let God.

To make the restoration process a little easier for me, Robert decided to be accountable for his whereabouts and encounters that normally he didn't feel the need to share. This helped a lot because he was trying to rebuild my trust. Although this seems overbearing for an adult, he thought his marriage was worth it. He committed to do whatever was necessary to salvage the qualities that were already established in our relationship. To rebuild our bond of trust, we spent extra time together discussing how we got to that state in our marriage. He said he felt isolated because I was so busy. I thought my busyness was justified because I was building a business. His feelings were valid, but I was still angry. I was young and didn't realize how to balance my career and take care of my husband and family. During that stage of my marriage, I thought he didn't have as much of a need. I guess I was wrong. I'm not blaming myself for his unfaithfulness, but he should have spoken up. Sometimes women can't read between the lines. It was totally up to me whether or not I would ever trust him again.

What does rebuilding trust look like in a broken marriage?

"But Jesus beheld them, and said unto them, with men this is impossible; but with God all things are possible" Matthew 19:26 (KJV).

You may say that you can forgive but you will never trust him. However, trust is analogous to forgiveness. You need the two of these characteristics in your marriage. Now let's be clear here. I am not saying you should be naïve and ignore any telltale signs that your husband is still actively violating your commitment. Trust does not mean you turn a blind eye, or you retreat into a state of denial. In

61

contrast, from a biblical perspective never get confused with how you should feel, and how you actually feel.

In the beginning stage I was absolutely bitter and defensive with people around me. First, I had to get over the anger because I didn't think he should be forgiven. Thankfully, understanding the Word of God allowed me to draw from the foundation that was instilled in me over the years. It was totally up to me whether or not I would ever trust him again. Although his responsibility for a lifetime was to give me every reason to trust him. After many years of hard work, he has re-established my trust. Every possible question I had he didn't hesitate to answer or prove his faithfulness to the marriage.

Prior to the consideration of rebuilding trust, the experience of side effects emotionally, mentally, physically, and spiritually was a great challenge. I saw life through different lenses. I lived for weeks in a confused state of mind. I was extremely frustrated because I could not predict the future. He was an excellent father, and I didn't want my children to be raised in a single-family home, although I was willing to make that decision if the infidelity was ongoing. I even questioned if it is possible for a man to be faithful. My husband was born again Christian. I had a lot of questions about mankind. Yes, with my "A" type personality I needed to get every question answered. I needed to know: the four (4) "W's" and the "how."

A. Who? - A married woman whose husband was unfaithful to her. She confessed that to me. She denied committing adultery with my husband.

B. What? - Adultery had taken place unfortunately. It was tough for me to even connect to that idea. In order to make a good decision I had to come to the realization that there was a long road ahead. Although I thought leaving would allow me to heal faster, staying could have a more positive outcome if he was extremely committed.

C. When - Ten years into our marriage. We were at the height of success. I was looking forward to growing and developing into more business. What a set-back, or shall I say a step moving forward.

D. Where - The other woman's office.

E. How - Cause and effect - Flirtatious conversation. Many people think flirtation is just harmless words that have no validity. Flirtation has caused so much disruption in peoples' lives. Oxford Dictionary states that "flirtation is behaving in such a way as to suggest a playful sexual attraction to someone."[7]

I thought it was important to mention this because trust can begin again once you know everything. Don't feel bad about wanting to know and don't allow your husband to skirt around answering the hard questions. Hold him accountable and express to him how important this is for you to build trust with him. Any man that wants to be with his wife and rebuild will do what he needs to help her become secure in the bond that they are rebuilding.

I started judging my appearance. I question things I wore or didn't wear. I knew I was confident but to be with someone who chose to explore other options caused me to judge whether or not he was attracted to me.

I just didn't understand if God had all power in His hand, why allow something so detrimental to happen to his daughter. I told God "I trusted you." Yes, past tense. I started to question the years that I have served God. Of all marriages, why did mine have to be the one that was broken? Again, we were both believers in Christ. Neither of us saw this coming. I felt like God betrayed me also. I thought I had enough faith in him to control man's thoughts and judgment. How could I think something so crazy? God has always given man the option to choose. I was innocently naïve. Yes, I was spiritually confused. The spirit of the Lord kept saying to me "I am so sorry this

---

[7] "Flirtatious English Definition," Lexico, Oxford, https://www.lexico.com/en/definition/flirtatious, (accessed 12/18/21)

has happened to you," as I sobbed. My thought was "God, I thought you loved me." God repeatedly told me that he was with me in my time of sorrow. Ten years into my marriage with three little children. I had no idea this would have been one of my mountains.

I was hurt and I wanted Robert to feel that same pain. After a few weeks I noticed my social skills subsided. I used to be the party girl in the family. Yes, in the spare moment I would call family and friends over for a spontaneous gathering (food, fun, fellowship). Everyone loved Bobby and Karen. It was said we were the ideal couple. I didn't want to be around family or friends. The shame was weighing on my heart. There was one thing on my mind; what to do with this situation. I was an emotional wreck. For months my emotions were so unstable. I felt insecure. I cried a lot. My heart felt like it was beyond repair, I thought. To think about divorcing made me feel that the world would view me as being a super independent woman. That would at least include who knows about the infidelity in addition to who didn't know. One minute I was on board with continuing in the relationship and the next minute I thought "am I being taken advantage of?" I constantly thought that my marriage was totally severed, but then seeing how Robert tried to mend all the broken pieces made me feel we had a good chance to survive this trauma.

Mentally I knew to immediately get therapy weekly, which helped stabilize my thoughts. There was a long road ahead to heal. Although I knew the adultery was not about me but how he felt about himself, whether low self-esteem or threatened manhood. Physically I wondered if I were pretty enough, was something inadequately disfigured on my body, etc. Likewise, I started considering my weight (130lbs), my hair stayed in tack, and I was young and vibrant. What would make him fall for another woman? Although this was unhealthy, I blamed myself. Maybe if I were a homemaker he would not have strayed. I was young and naïve.

At this time, I started to have trust issues with God because I had prayed for a husband and he betrayed me. I had to process through that and understand God had nothing to do with Robert's decision to sin. God was my only secure source. I desperately needed to hear from him and feel his love.

I felt like no one really understood what I was going through because they had never experienced that type of betrayal. Being in the church community holds a different dynamic than the values of the world. In the world, people have all types of compromised relationships, but the children of God roadmap abide by the word of God. We sought after every scripture possible to find some refuge and consolation. Our lives can get too busy and chaotic. Then we become disconnected to the spiritual path we should be on. These two scriptures are great for reconnecting and finding your way on a new path.

"For husbands, this means love your wives, just as Christ loved the church. He gave up his life for her." Ephesians: 5:25 (NLT).

"Therefore shall a man leave his father and his mother, and shall cleave unto his wife: and they shall be one flesh (Genesis 2:24 KJV).

My trust was shifted but I held onto my faith that God would see me through this, even though it looked grim. I had to learn to trust the voice of God again.

There's No Space or Place Like Home

Hello Karen,

I realize that what I did was impulsive and extremely reckless. I'm humbly grateful to have you as my wife. I know that what I created was a situation that would have been a disaster for my being if you hadn't extended your forgiveness and mercy towards me. I would have destroyed and lost the best thing that God has allowed me to gracefully experience, that is my marriage to you. I assure you that I'm sorry for the pain and agony I caused you. It was tough to see you sob from the aches and pain of betrayal. What I brought unto you was terrible, and you didn't deserve it. I honestly considered this torment as self-infliction, which I remorsefully regret to an enormous great degree. My regrettable emotions are so devastating and cannot be expressed with words to even just describe. I never would've wanted to see you suffer from what I did; as quoted in Ephesians 5:28-29 KJV...

So ought men to love their wives as their own bodies. He that loveth his wife loveth himself.

For no man ever yet hated his own flesh; but nourisheth and cherisheth it, even as the Lord the church.

I, therefore, will earnestly spend the rest of my life with the purpose of restoration and making up for such an act of disloyalty that broke your trust in me. I love you, adore and respect the innocence we once had. I decided that forever I will treat you as if I just met you. I will never allow myself to be comfortable unless I'm confident that you are comfortable and secure from now on and forever. You are my best friend, and like I always say when I see you or just greet you when you call me, and I answer the phone, "Hey GIRLFRIEND."

I have no excuses and seek after none. But, I will say that the two years of shared therapy sessions we endured and spent together were so illuminating. It allowed me to see and understand how my history and growing from childhood to adolescence on into adulthood experiences formed dysfunctional behaviors that cause shame in the eyes of truth and honor. So, transforming is rewarding and creates peace and happiness that I never knew. There is a joy that awaits us through shedding and purging from iniquity, and it is immeasurably awesome. The results bring you a warm and welcoming home. There's no space or place like home.

Family is the foundation of everything that happiness is built upon. You are my soul mate, and the enemy would want that to be destroyed. Thanks again for not giving up on me. The song writer's words best describe my pathway when he sang the song, "I once was lost, but now I'm found, I was blind, but now I see."

Yours truly,
Robert

CHAPTER EIGHT

Get Over It? Really!!

The hardest decision you will make through this process is should you stay and work on your marriage or you should leave. This is a personal decision between you and God so don't let anyone, including your spouse and kids, influence your decision.

People may say, "Girl, get over it; at least he comes home every night." Reality check! Just because a man comes home every night doesn't mean he's not thinking about someone else in his heart. Whatever you decide to do, don't settle. If the Bible releases you from adultery, I believe that God knows the pain and He understands the effect adultery can have on you. He never wanted divorces, but He knew man would have a hardened heart. Again, I repeat if there's something to work with, try to work through it. Just do not minimize the destruction from this type of abuse.

My Self-Care Retreat (continued)

The next day at the resort, I had my itinerary at the front door of my cabin. The events were really nice including water aerobics, swimming, workouts, yoga, and extensive walking trails. Nature walking was my favorite. Sitting in the meditation room, I gave myself permission to be hurt and confused. I did not have it all together, and it was okay. I constantly reminded myself that I would rise above this problem. Starting to think from the beginning of how we met made me smile. What went wrong? After the trip, I told Robert that I agreed to work on our marriage.

When I went back home, Robert and I had another appointment with the therapist. She asked me if I had made a decision to continue in the relationship.

"Yes, I have."

"Look at him, and tell him the decision," she said.

"Robert, I will try to the best of my ability to hang in here with you, but it may be a long, hard journey. I don't know what lies ahead of us, but I am willing to take the risk." We were looking directly into one another's eyes.

Responding, he said, "Karen, I will spend the rest of my life making this up to you. I may not be perfect in every other area, but I will never be in this situation again."

I knew we were headed for some serious healing and rebuilding, but we both had to decide about whether we would fight for the home or not. Experts say it's possible for couples to go on to have a happy relationship after infidelity, provided they're willing to put in the work. "The couple can survive and grow after an affair."

[8]It would have been easier if I had decided to exit my marriage. The truth is, I was financially stable and would not have to take the risk of rebuilding my life. My quality of life would not change if my husband walked away. My financial portfolio in addition to my large childcare center business would have allowed me to raise my children as an independent mother. I was surrounded by affluent business colleagues. I mention this because many women choose to stay because of finances. I did not choose to stay because I was codependent on his income. I stayed because I wanted to work on my

---

[8] Korin Miller; Meredith Clark, "Why Some Couples Can Recover After Cheating and Others Can't," Self, December 27th, 2018, https://www.self.com/story/why-some-couples-can-recover-after-cheating-and-others-cant, (accessed 12/18/21)

marriage. Despite what he had done, I had to admit that Robert had more good qualities than bad.

The Holy Spirit guided me in my decisions as that inner voice spoke to me and told me that I would be making a big mistake if I left. God let me know I was free to exit my marriage if I wanted to. We had so many great qualities as a couple. Although he was unfaithful to me, I never stopped loving Robert.

Should you decide to stay you will need to rebuild your relationship brick by brick. Some of you may choose to stay because you feel there's no way out. Perhaps due to a lack of financial resources. I'm not advising or persuading you to exit your marriage, but there are resources to reconstruct your life. Likewise, there are resources if you want to thrive in your relationship.

Seek Therapy

I know there are situations when our men think they do not need therapy. Pray diligently about this and move on. Go to therapy for yourself if needed. Don't worry about whether you will have to leave your husband or not; just work on the whole you. Robert and I understood that we would have to invest some valuable time if we wanted to mend broken pieces in the marriage. We sought after a highly reputable therapist. Although we could not make it without the Holy Spirit's help, we needed therapy as a couple and individually. Throughout the therapy sessions, we did individual counseling and couples' sessions. It was very emotional. We were able to get to the nucleus of our problem. Unbelievably, most of them stemmed from our childhood experiences. Also, we were taught through therapy to communicate with purpose. Robert allowed me to ask as many questions as possible that I needed answers to. Sometimes it was cumbersome, but he was in it for the longevity of the marriage.

One Step at a Time

It was critical that we rebuild our relationship by spending more time together. We established date night every week. Phones down, no children, and we did not discuss problems, or finances. We couldn't believe how much this helped us. It was amazing! Robert and I looked forward to Date Night. We still abide by Date Night after thirty-one years of marriage. Also, we surround ourselves with other Kingdom marriages. Approximately two to four couples. We shared challenges, laughs, dreams, and set goals, while supporting one another. Nothing could keep us together but prayer.

Being Intimate Again

Before the infidelity I thought our intimate time was okay. It was not necessarily great because I was extremely busy and very focused on my endeavors, I must admit. Being extremely busy can be challenging on a healthy sex life. At the time I didn't give it much thought. Again, I was much younger during the time of betrayal. I've come to know that maintaining healthy sexual activity is just as important as every other aspect of the relationship.

We didn't connect sexually immediately after the adultery. At the time I felt like I didn't want him anymore. I must mention our love making was almost obsolete. Our intimacy was compromised temporarily. Of course, the first time we connected intimately after the infidelity, we hugged so tightly as if to never let go. There was a new appreciation of each other. We realized we could lose each other in a moment. Life is so fragile, and we must have an appreciation and respect for what God joins together. In other words, don't take each other for granted.

When the trust was broken subconsciously, I felt like a third person was in my bedroom. After reconnecting mentally, spiritually, and physically, that subsided, then we were able to re-establish a healthy sex life. There are many ways to rebuild that intimacy. It also helped me with trusting him again. You must *connect* during lovemaking. You must be present.

"For this cause shall a man leave his father and mother, and shall be joined unto his wife, and they two shall be one flesh." (Ephesians 5:31 KJV)

"This is a great mystery: but I speak concerning Christ and the church." Ephesians 5:32 (KJV)

Take Care of Yourself

Self-care means to care for oneself by having all his/her needs met. If you have never seen self-care as a child, this may be a difficult transition for you. It is actually a learned behavior you may have been exposed to in your childhood years. As a child, although my mom was married, she worked very hard. She was definitely the virtuous woman the Bible speaks about. What I learned from her was to work extremely hard and deny yourself while putting family before your needs.

In the beginning stages of my marriage, I thought I could do it all. I was young, vibrant, and enthusiastic about marriage. I wanted to be the best wife a man could ever desire. Likewise, the best mother my children would admire. In addition, that bold, resilient businesswoman colleagues looked up to. I must include my spiritual walk, which was most popular and respected in the church. Therefore, I did it all and at the same time.

I truthfully inherited those traits. As I matured and developed into womanhood, I recognized there were needs that were not met. I would purchase every self-help book that would answer some of the questions I had and take my pretty journal into my prayer closest to capture thoughts and write what God spoke to me. Amazingly it worked.

In order to clarify the true meaning of self-care, I have listed some steps to consider when caring for yourself.

Mental Self-care - Talk to a close friend, therapist, or spiritual leader. Journal daily. Get at least 7 to 8 hours of sleep. Rebuke negative thoughts.

Physical Self-care - Take a walk to your favorite places to visit or your neighborhood. Take a warm bath while reading your favorite book. Sip on a cup of warm green tea with antioxidants. Drink water. Eat balanced meals, eliminating salty snacks with high preservatives. Yoga, workout, or join a fitness group. Soak in sunlight. Walk at least 30 -45 minutes a day. Have lunch with the girls.

Spiritual Self-care - Give thanks for five minutes a day. Pray. Patiently wait to hear God speak to you. Sit in his presence. Listen to your heart. Read spiritual material.

As you are going through your healing process, try to minimize your responsibilities, if possible, to invest in more self-care and journaling. Ask God to guide you through your decision making. Self-care is doing the things that bring you happiness, like having lunch with a close friend, seeking individual therapy, or even taking a couple of days to a retreat alone. Sit with your feelings and don't let anyone try to confuse you on how you should feel. Listen to the heart. It never lies. Your future is brighter whether you decide to stay or disconnect with your husband. God our Father will never leave you nor forsake you (Hebrew 13:5). He will always send you the support you need to get through tough times.

CHAPTER NINE

Coming Out Smelling Like a Bed of Roses

A healthy marriage can be one of the greatest experiences in life. It's one of the most intimate relationships you will ever experience where you share your life's joys and sorrows. There are amazing memories to talk about as the marriage develops. Marriage is at its best when the two are selfless.

Now my life has finally gotten back on track. Although the road I walk with Robert will never be the same, I feel that it is a good thing. I am very clear on the basis of continuing our relationship and so is he. I know that if I had kept moving along in the relationship without confrontation, it would have grown really ugly. But our relationship has surprisingly grown tremendously from this.

Today I work hard at keeping a balance for my family. God first, home second, and business endeavors last. This formula does balance me. During the healing process, I never let go of my dreams. I wrote them down, and they are coming to pass. I knew early on that dreams can have a way of disappearing when you're in a crisis. But, regardless of what goes on in your life, never stop dreaming. Sometimes that's all you have to hold on to. Find a good friend to share your ideas with. You will be keeping hope alive.

Also, it's always good to be under strong leadership at your church with pastors who practice the moral structure and faithfulness for families. Besides, families carry the weight of the church body.

God says if two or three are gathered in his name, there he is in the midst. There were many days when Robert and I prayed for ourselves out of trouble or for healing for other couples. We don't have to be defeated by Satan, throwing our relationships away. There is hope after adultery. Of the couples who choose to work through this problem, over fifty percent of their relationships grow stronger after this. To my Christian brothers and sisters, don't live in shame or despair; you are not the only one going through this as a Christian family.

As time goes on, I feel good about the choices I have made for the healing I needed for this calamity. Yes, I do identify this as a calamity, although others may minimize the impact it can have on an individual. I just chose to go on the long journey of healing to refrain from being another case of a depressed woman needing medication to cope in a very dysfunctional situation.

I smell freshly cut roses. The fragrance of life is such a sweet smell. Realizing how God brought me through this trial without losing my sanity made me want to save as many relationships as possible. I never thought I could survive betrayal but slowing down to smell those roses caused great healing in areas I never considered to be shattered.

I did come out smelling like a full bed of colorful roses. You will also. It doesn't matter whether or not the relationship survived. The most important thing is that you did not lose your mind.

You see, I associate the rose with women because the characteristics are so comparable. The rose is a high-maintenance plant. There are various types of roses, such as heritage and antique. These are tough and will grow through most stresses. Many roses have been found left alone in deadly places but yet still thrive. Research states that if planted in the right spot, heritage roses should provide years of healthy growth and beautiful blooms. They have been proven to be disease resistant. With heritage roses, none of the fungus diseases debilitates them. They just drop the affected leaves and grow through the disease. Various roses do require some pruning.

The point I'm trying to make is that roses are a symbolization of the female species. We do have a strong reputation for being high maintenance. Although we look like glamor girls on our outer appearances, we need to maintain within. So high-maintenance is taking care of the whole you—mind, body, and soul.

Some roses, like victimized women, will grow through many stresses. Think about it. Many women have been left unattended, but like strong roses, are survivors, and have thrived through the neglect and abuse.

Many diseases have spread across the nation due to strongholds on our minds and being held captive by our significant others. But we were not built to carry so many female physical problems. The rose is not prone to diseases because it allows itself to keep growing. Unfortunately, we normally stop our lives and pay more attention to changing our mates than taking care of ourselves. Once the mind is distraught, then the body stresses and escalates to diabetes, high blood pressure, weight gain, etc. Like the roses, you can survive these stresses if they are dealt with early on. We must take care of our inner self. A good start is to realize you are only responsible for yourself and your actions. You cannot change or manipulate your mate into doing what you feel is best.

In my situation, I chose to re-evaluate my life. Looking within myself, I realized how bloody my heart had become. Immediately I knew that we would have to separate or go through an extremely long healing process. I remember telling Robert not to buy me roses after the adultery because my sense of smell was traumatized.

May God heal the hurt that has changed your life. I know everyone does not come out of this alive. For those of you who have experienced this, you can make it through this crisis. Just be sure to process your decision before giving up. Follow your heart. No one will ever know your mate like you do. So, it is very difficult to base your decision of staying in your relationship on others' opinions. Every day is an inch to re-establish trust. Hold on! Don't give up!

Dear Friend,
   I love you immensely with the love of Christ. My friend, when you hurt, I hurt. When you cry, I shed tears along with you. I know your pain. Our story may be different, but the intense pain is familiar. Prophetically, I see strength within you. You shall win. Your life is created for greatness. You are seeking help and self-care but unsure of where to turn. You may have a deaf ear due to betrayal, but God will never leave you nor forsake you. Yes, He's in the trenches alongside you. That humiliation, shame, low self-esteem, depression, and rejection you feel, God is there. It may be unimaginable right now, but you will share that beautiful smile again. You can make it through this just as God transitioned you through many other situations. I understand that you have many unanswered questions. You are probably asking God why this challenge? Furthermore, why me? In this life, everything has been purposed. Our scars are pivoted for Kingdom building. Challenges you thought you were not equipped for, nor prepared for, God is still in control and will be glorified. Yes, God says this hurt is not to destroy you but that He may be glorified in how He delivers you.
   Please know that you are beautiful, powerful, and a mighty gift to the Kingdom of God. I know this pain feels unbearable but be steadfast in prayer every morning. Focus on what you need, and how you feel. Remember who you are. God calls you friend. John 15:15 KJV, "Henceforth I call you not servants; for the servant knoweth not what his lord doeth: but I have called you friends; for all things that I have heard of my Father I have made known unto you." I am praying with you. I am praying for you.

Proverbs 31:10 – 31 (KJV)

31:10 Who can find a virtuous woman for her price is far above rubies.

31:11 The heart of her husband doth safely trust in her, so that he shall have no need of spoil.

31:12 She will do him good and not evil all the days of her life.

31:13 She seeketh wool, and flax, and worketh willingly with her hands.

31:14 She is like the merchants' ships; she bringeth her food from afar.

31:15 She riseth also while it is yet night, and giveth meat to her household, and a portion to her maidens.

31:16 She considereth a field, and buyeth it: with the fruit of her hands, she planteth a vineyard.

31:17 She girdeth her loins with strength, and strengtheneth her arms.

31:18 She perceiveth that her merchandise is good: her candle goeth not out by night.

31:19 She layeth her hands to the spindle, and her hands hold the distaff.

31:20 She stretcheth out her hand to the poor; yea, she reacheth forth her hands to the needy.

31:21 She is not afraid of the snow for her household: for all her household are clothed with scarlet.

31:22 She maketh herself coverings of tapestry; her clothing is silk and purple.

31:23 Her husband is known in the gates, when he sitteth among the elders of the land.

31:24 She maketh fine linen, and selleth it; and delivereth girdles unto the merchant.

31:25 Strength and honor are her clothing; and she shall rejoice in time to come.

31:26 She openeth her mouth with wisdom; and in her tongue is the law of kindness.

31:27 She looketh well to the ways of her household, and eateth not the bread of idleness.

31:28 Her children arise up, and call her blessed; her husband also, and he praiseth her.

31:29 Many daughters have done virtuously, but thou excellest them all.

31:30 Favour is deceitful, and beauty is vain: but a woman that feareth the LORD, she shall be praised.

31:31 Give her of the of her hands; and let her own works praise her in the gates.

The "Virtuous Woman" you are. May God grace you with his rich Blessings. May God's peace be upon you.

●

Love,

Karen Michele

ACKNOWLEDGMENTS

I would like to thank my husband and soul mate Pastor Robert Butler. You are truly my best friend. You are an amazing "Man of God".

Special thanks to my amazing three children, Charity, Christen, and Robert II. I am so blessed to have the opportunity to raise such compassionate and supportive children.

Minister Suzette Perry, you have truly been the strength and foundation for all my accomplishments. Thank you for seeing life through positive lenses. You are a testament of the power of prayer.

To Angela Womack, a dear friend to me and Robert who have supported me throughout many years.

Although I cannot recognize everyone who had an intricate part in writing this book I must thank Dr. Sherrie Walton, CEO of Walton Publishing House for her enthusiasm and tenacity in keeping me on task until the book was completed.

About the Author

Karen Butler is an Author, Business Strategist, Co-Pastor, Life Coach, wife of 32 years, Mom of three wonderful adult children, and Grandma of one grandson. She started her early career establishing a large Childcare Center with an enrollment of 110 children. After serving in ministry for many years, she and Robert started a grassroot church in Leesburg, Va.

Karen Michele assists marriages with tools and techniques through workshops, conferences, and one on one coaching. Married couples must sometimes reset the trajectory in which the relationship is going to get the positive end results. She believes that marriages should thrive through prayer and hard work.

Let's get connected!

Website: www.ifyouseemyhusband.com
For bookings: info@ifyouseemyhusband.com